CONTEMPORARY'S

New Beginnings in Reading

BOOK 2

Bonnie Tivenan

Edited by
David Caes

CB

CONTEMPORARY
BOOKS

CHICAGO

Contents

The illustrations of the front covers of *Why Johnny Can't Read* by Rudolf Flesch (New York: Harper and Brothers, 1955) and *On Learning to Read: The Child's Fascination with Meaning* by Bruno Bettelheim and Karen Zelan (New York: Knopf, 1982) are used by permission of Harper & Row, Publishers, Inc., and Alfred A. Knopf, Inc.

Consultants
Elaine Belz, M.Ed.
Chad Consuegra, M.S.W.
Rhoda Konigsberg
Susan Paull

The author would like to thank Sandra Stewart, Kate Lindsey, Iris Saltiel, and Pat Boos for their help and valuable suggestions. She would also like to acknowledge Louise Craft, Sandra Pak, and Lois Patton, of Teachers College Press staff, for their invaluable assistance with the first edition. Finally, the author would like to acknowledge Lillie May Hadley and Doane Hadley of Attache Business Service, who worked many hours on the word processor.

The illustrator would like to acknowledge Kenneth Shore.

Cover photo © H. Armstrong Roberts

Editorial Director
Caren Van Slyke

Production Editor
Patricia Reid

Art and Production
Princess Louise El
Arvid Carlson

Typography
David Fultz

Cover photo © Michael Slaughter

Published by Contemporary Books, Inc., Two Prudential Plaza, Chicago, Illinois 60601-6790, (312) 540-4500

Published simultaneously in Canada by Fitzhenry & Whiteside, 195 Allstate Parkway, Markham, Ontario L3R 4T8 Canada

Copyright © 1991, 1985 by Bonnie Tivenan

ISBN: 0-8092-5175-2

Manufactured in the United States of America

Notes to the Instructor*

PHILOSOPHY BEHIND THE PROGRAM

This program was designed with adult and adolescent beginning readers in mind. It readily lends itself to use with students who are low-level readers.

It is essential that adult beginning readers redefine themselves as being capable of learning to read. *New Beginnings* provides a framework for successful experiences by providing small skill increments and large amounts of repetition. But more important than mere repetition or small increments is the nature of the readings and exercises. They have been written with the assumption that the students are the intellectual equals of the author and the instructor. As students redefine themselves as intellectually competent, they come to view themselves as being capable of mastering the reading process. In addition, the subject matter of even the earliest exercises should be of interest to the adult student.

A COMPLETE LITERACY PROGRAM FOR THE ADULT BEGINNING READER

New Beginnings in Reading offers quality instruction, high-interest reading material, and ample reinforcement exercises for beginning readers (levels 0–3). Its integrated phonics, sight words, and structural analysis/decoding skills approach enables learners to key into their most effective and comfortable learning styles.

Each book in this nine-book developmental series builds on the skills and vocabulary presented in prior texts. Instructional material is introduced and reinforced in small skill increments and a variety of practice exercises, allowing learners to work independently or in group settings.

A CLOSER LOOK AT NEW BEGINNINGS' INSTRUCTIONAL COMPONENTS

Placement Test—accurately locates where students should begin study in the program

Groundbreaker Exercises—the starting point for students with limited sight vocabulary, phonics, and decoding skills

Odd-Numbered Books (1, 3, 5, 7)—weave instruction with life-skills oriented topics (e.g., health, consumer economics, employment, housing)

Even-Numbered Books (2, 4, 6, 8)—use topics that identify and elaborate on the goals and experiences of literacy students (e.g., lesson 5 in each of the even-numbered books in the series contains personal accounts from several beginning readers)

Instructor's Guide—for both tutors and professionals; includes thorough instructional guidelines, teaching and motivational strategies, and walk-throughs of all lesson types characteristic of each book in the series

EXERCISES AND READINGS

New Beginnings in Reading—Book 2 contains five lessons that build on the concepts and skills developed in previous books in *New Beginnings*. Each lesson has a similar format. This consistency aids beginning students, who are often confused by diverse layouts and exercises.

Section titles are accompanied either by circles or by stars. Those with circles (●) require instructor assistance; those with stars (★) can be carried out independently by the students when they become familiar with the format. Every exercise has a footnote giving instructions to the instructor.

Each lesson in Book 2 is made up of nine different sections:

● New Words ●

DIRECTIONS: The instructor reads each new word and the first sentence of each accompanying pair of sentences. The student reads the second sentence.
PURPOSE: To introduce the student to new vocabulary words by presenting words in isolation as well as in context.

● Reading Selection ●

DIRECTIONS: The student reads the passage with assistance from the instructor, if that is necessary.
PURPOSE: To reinforce the new vocabulary.

---

*The Instructor's Guide elaborates on the philosophy behind *New Beginnings*. It also describes the series in much more detail.

★ Quiz for Reading Selection ★

DIRECTIONS: The student reads and answers these comprehension questions to see how well he or she understands what is being read. Once he or she is familiar with these pages, they can be assigned as independent work, at the discretion of the instructor.
PURPOSE: To reinforce old and new vocabulary.

MORE READING

At the end of the book there is a story that can be assigned as independent work. In addition to providing reinforcement, the story can be used to demonstrate to the student his or her increased reading competence.

● Tips on How to Improve Your Reading ●

DIRECTIONS: The instructor reads these tips to the student. The instructor and the student may discuss these techniques.
PURPOSE: To make the student an equal in the teaching and learning process, while sharing useful information with him or her.

● Skill Building ●

DIRECTIONS: The instructor reads the instructions to the student, who then carries them out by reading the exercises and filling in the blanks.
PURPOSE OF EACH SECTION
   A. To teach the student how to use the meaning of a sentence to identify a word.
   B. To identify compound words.
   C. To teach the use of known words to identify unknown words.
   D. To teach the use of word shapes in identifying words.
   E. To reinforce new vocabulary and teach the student how to use the meaning of a sentence to help identify a word.
   F. To teach the suffix -er.
   G. To reinforce old vocabulary words.
   H. To identify words that have more than one meaning and show the student how to use and define these words.

★ Reading to Know Others ★

DIRECTIONS: This reading can be assigned for independent work at the instructor's discretion.
PURPOSE: To reinforce old and new vocabulary.

● Time to Write ●

DIRECTIONS: The instructor reads the instructions to the student, who then reads the model(s) and writes his or her own composition.
PURPOSE: To reinforce reading skills through a structured language experience activity.

● Sounding It Out ●

DIRECTIONS: The instructor reads the instructions to the student. The student reads and completes the exercises.
PURPOSE: To introduce basic phonics patterns and to identify the word families based on those patterns.

★ On Your Own ★

DIRECTIONS: These plays, stories, and other exercises can be assigned as independent work.
PURPOSE: To reinforce old and new vocabulary and give the student an opportunity to work on his or her own.

FLASH CARDS

DIRECTIONS: The instructor should show the student how to use the pictorial and context cues on the backs of the cards before assigning them. Specific directions are included with the cards.
PURPOSE: To reinforce new vocabulary.

ANSWER KEY

DIRECTIONS: If appropriate, the instructor can have the student correct his or her own work.
PURPOSE: To allow the student to correct his or her own work, providing the student with a sense of independence. This also makes correcting assignments easier for the instructor.

WORD LIST, PLACEMENT TEST, PRETEST

The word list, the Placement Test, and the pretest all serve the same purpose. Any of them can be used to determine whether Book 2 is the appropriate book in *New Beginnings* for a particular student. If the separate placement test is not available, the instructor can use the pretest on page v to determine if Book 2 is an appropriate place for the student to begin work. Criteria for placement in Book 2 or advancement to Book 3 is included at the bottom of the pretest. If, for some reason, the student cannot be tested, the instructor can review the word list on pages 81 and 82 to determine if Book 2 is appropriate for the student.

GETTING READY, POSTTEST, AND CERTIFICATE OF MASTERY

Getting Ready can be used to help a student review the vocabulary words in Book 2 in preparation for the posttest.
The posttest (page 84) and Certificate of Mastery (page 85) should be used to celebrate the student's increased competence. If additional reinforcement exercises are indicated by the posttest, the presentation of the Certificate of Mastery should be followed by additional activities recommended in the Instructor's Guide.

Book 2 Pretest

(35 sight words and short **i**)

EXERCISE 1:   Read this letter.

Jan. 3, 1942

To my baby girl,

You are my first child. And I want to tell you many, many things. About me. About your mother. About why we had you. And about the way I feel about you.

At first I was afraid of you. I did not know what you wanted or what to do for you. You and your mother were good teachers. But I learned slowly.

But then you went from being a baby to being a little girl. We played. You sat on my lap. I read to you. We made things.

And you used to come to me and ask me to tell you a story. But you did not want one story. You always wanted more and more. But I have no more time for stories. And I have some important things to say to you.

I have to go to war. And I may or may not come back. When you are an adult, you will read what I wrote. And as an adult I want to tell you some things.

I believe that a woman can do anything she wants to do. If she wants to get married that is OK, but she can do other things too. If you want to be president, you can do it. If you want to write books, do it. Live the way you want to live. Be who you want to be. The world can be a good place.

I will always love you,

Dad

EXERCISE 2:   Say these sounds.

ig   ip   ick   it   id   ill   im   in   ib   ix   iss

PRETEST DIRECTIONS: Read the instructions to the student. If a student misses six or more words or appears to be frustrated, discontinue the pretest. After explaining that these words will be taught in Book 2, proceed to Exercise 2. Record the short vowel sounds that the student has difficulty with. If a student misses 6 or more words, begin work in Lesson 1. If the student misses fewer than six words, teach him or her the words and short vowel sounds missed and then proceed to the pretest in Book 3.

v

MANY PEOPLE CANNOT READ

• Things to Think About When You Read Lesson 1 •

NEW WORDS

1. come
20,000,000 people in the U.S.A. cannot read as well as they want to.
How **come**?

2. way
How many **ways** can teachers teach reading?
What are the **ways**?

3. or
Is 6, 9, 11 **or** 13 the best time for learning to read?
Or is 25, 35, or 45 the best time?

4. good
Is it **good** for a child to go to 3 or more schools?
Is it **good** for a child to go to 1 or 2 schools?

5. who
Who do the schools teach the best?
Who learns the best?

6. of
Are reading teachers the best teachers **of** reading?
Or are other teachers the best teachers **of** reading?

7. more
When will the schools have **more** reading teachers?
When will the schools have **more** money?

NEW WORDS: The instructor reads the new word and the first sentence of each pair. The student reads the second sentence of each pair. (Throughout the lessons circles appear next to the title of exercises that require instructor assistance.)

The U.S.A. has 237,000,000 people.

Of the 237,000,000 people in the U.S.A.,
67,000,000 can read a little.

Of the 237,000,000 people in the U.S.A.,
20,000,000 cannot read as well as they want to.

Most schools give children 1 time to learn to read. The time is when the children are little. Little children do not see how important reading is.

Most children come to school when they are 5. And most schools teach all children to read when they are 6. For some children, 6 is not a good time for learning to read. Sometimes 7, 9, 11, or 13 is the best time for learning to read. Many schools do not look at what is best for the child. They think 6 is **the** time.

Schools can use 3 ways to teach reading. Sometimes they use 1 way and not the other 2. Sometimes the way the school teaches is not the best way for a child to learn. Sometimes the child can learn with another way. But the school does not teach the other way.

2 schools can teach 2 ways of learning to read. 1 school can teach 1 way. 1 school can teach another way. When a child goes to 2 schools, he may not learn 1 way or the other.

Some children who are 9, 10, or 11 have reading teachers. But many children who are 9, 10 or 11 have teachers who do not teach reading well. They may or may not know how to teach reading.

The U.S.A. has 237,000,000 people.

Of the 237,000,000 people in the U.S.A.,
67,000,000 can read a little.

Of the 237,000,000 people in the U.S.A.,
20,000,000 cannot read as well as they want to.

READING SELECTION: The student reads the passage with instructor assistance, if necessary.

A.   Write your own title for the story.

_____

> **Good readers** sometimes read a story 2 or 3 times in order to answer questions correctly.

B.   From the story, decide if the statements are true. Circle **Yes** or **No**.

   1.   All teachers can teach reading.   Yes   No

   2.   Many schools say 11 is the time to learn to read.   Yes   No

   3.   6 is the best time for all children to learn to read.   Yes   No

   4.   Schools can use 3 ways to teach reading.   Yes   No

C.   What do you think?   Circle One

   1.   Most schools are good.   Yes   No   Maybe

   2.   Most teachers are good.   Yes   No   Maybe

   3.   Going to 3 schools is a good thing for a child.   Yes   No   Maybe

D.   Write what you think.

   1.   Reading is _____

       _____

   2.   Going to school is _____

       _____

QUIZ: If necessary, assist the student with exercises A and D. When the student is comfortable with this exercise, similar exercises in later lessons can be assigned as independent work. The answer key is on page 77.

• Tips on How to Improve Your Reading •

Becoming a good reader means learning to do more than one thing at a time. At the same time a good reader is looking at the shape and letters in a word, he or she is also looking to be sure that the sentence makes sense. If a sentence does not make sense, the good reader goes back to the word that seems wrong and tries to read it again.

In some ways learning to read is like learning to drive a car. In reading and in driving you have to know how to do many things at once. In the beginning you may have difficulty doing several things at once. With time and practice, it will become much easier.

• Skill Building •

A. Think of a word to complete the sentence. Then write it.

Many people cannot read.
Many have not learned to read at all.

Some people have learned to _____ a little.

You are going to read about schools, teachers, and learning _____ read.

B. Each of these words is a combination of 2 words. Circle each of the 2 words inside the big one.

1. boyfriend   2. become

C. Add a letter to the word you already know. Say and write the new word.

for   NEW WORD

for + t = _____

for + m = _____

D. Put each word in the shape that fits it.

who
or
of

TIPS: Read these tips to the student and discuss them with him or her.
SKILL BUILDING: Read the lettered instructions to the student. The answer key is on page 77.

Good readers make sure every sentence makes sense.

E. Read each sentence and write the word that completes it.

way   or   come   good   who   more   of

1. I have to have m _ _ _ money.

2. Matt is a g _ _ _ man.

3. Are you going my w _ _?

4. I want you to c _ _ _ with me.

5. O _ all my friends, you are the best.

6. Can you tell me w _ _ she is?

7. Are the boys o _ girls going?

F. Add an **er** ending to make "one who does something."

1. He likes to _____.
    fight fighter

2. He is a good _____.
    fight fighter

3. She wants to become a _____.
    teach teacher

4. He likes to _____.
    teach teacher

G. Read the sentence. Then write the words that are in **bold print**.

I talk to **them**.
I play with them.
I read to them.
Then I nap.

th_____   th_____

H. Circle the word that is repeated each time you see it.

1. How come?   2. He lives at 234 Old Friends Way.

    Will you come to the house?   Can you tell me the way?

DIRECTIONS: Exercise F shows how **er** can be added to a word to show "one who does something" or a doer.
ADDITIONAL REINFORCEMENT: When the student is comfortable with the new words in this lesson, the flash cards at the end of the book can be used for reinforcement.

Ann writes:

I have had good teachers. And I have had some bad teachers.

I had 1 teacher that I did not like. Not at all. And she did not like me. Mrs. M. was not old. But she was fat. And I liked to make her mad. I wasted time. And she yelled. I played with the boys. And she yelled. I had fights with the girls. And she yelled.

But then I had Mrs. Fat. She was the best. She liked me. And I loved her. I played quietly for her. I read. I worked. I learned.

I know that having a good teacher is important. But I think teachers are like other people. Some are good at what they do. Some are not. I know when I have a good teacher. But I do not know what makes a good teacher.

WHAT ABOUT YOU?

Have you had some good teachers?

What were they like?

Have you had some bad teachers?

What were they like?

Have you had more good or more bad teachers?

What makes a teacher good or bad?

READING TO KNOW OTHERS: This exercise can be assigned for independent work.
REMINDER: Flash cards for the new words are located at the end of the book and can be used at the instructor's discretion.

Read the letter to Ann and her answer. Then read the letter addressed to you and write your answer to it.

Letter to Ann

Ann,
    Do you think all people can become good readers? Do they have to go to school? Do they have to have a teacher?

> Someone Who Wants
> to Become a Good
> Reader

Answer from Ann

Someone,
    I *know* that all people can become good readers. At 1 time I was not a good reader. But I learned. And if I can do it, other people can too.
    You do not have to go to school to become a good reader. But you do have to have a good teacher. And you do have to do 3 things: 1) read 2) read, and 3) read.

> Ann

Letter to you

Do you think I can become a good reader? How can I become a good reader?

> I Want to Be
> a Good Reader

Answer from you

Reader,

_____

_____

_____

_____

_____

_____

DIRECTIONS: Read the instructions to the students. Encourage the students to write their own answers, but assist them with spelling any words that they need help with. Reassure any student who has difficulty with the exercise that copying the model word for word is quite appropriate. If the student hesitates to write, the student should dictate his or her letter to the instructor. The instructor should write the letter on a separate piece of paper and then let the student copy it into the book.

ĭ =

A. Circle the picture of all words that begin with the ĭ sound.

ĭ

ĭ

B. Fill in the blank to spell the word.

1. r __ b
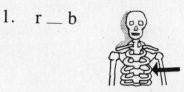

2. k __ ss

3. l __ ps

C. Read words with the ĭ sound in sentences.

1. He **is in** the house.
2. I **will** go **if** you go.
3. He loves **his children**.

D. Use the words with the ĭ sound in sentences.

1. He played with _____ friends.
   in his

2. I am _____ school.
   in if

3. She will play _____ I play.
   in if

SOUNDING IT OUT: Read the instructions for each section to the student. The answer key for exercises B through H is on page 77.

E. Circle the words that make the ĭ sound.

think   will   like   is   girl   children

F. Read the following sounds and words.

id		**ill**	
ĭ	bid	ĭ	bill
ĭ	did	ĭ	fill
ĭ	hid	ĭ	hill
ĭ	kid	ĭ	Jill
ĭ	lid	ĭ	kill
ĭ	rid	ĭ	mill
ĭ	Sid	ĭ	pill
		ĭ	till
		ĭ	will

1. Think of a sentence for each of the above words. Then say it.

2. Use the words above to fill in the blanks.

    a. He h __ __ the money.

    b. I w __ __ __ see my brother.

    c. He is a good k __ __.

    d. S __ __ wastes money.

    e. She d __ __ not go.

    f. Do you have money for the b __ __ __?

    g. J __ __ __ is the boss.

3. Spell the words on the lines below as they are said to you.

id	**ill**
a. _____	a. _____
b. _____	b. _____
c. _____	c. _____
d. _____	d. _____
e. _____	e. _____

G.   Circle the sentence that describes the picture.

1.
   a. Bill hid the will.
   b. Bill killed Jill.
   c. Bill loves Jill.

2.
   a. The kid did not go.
   b. The kid has the lid.
   c. The kid likes Sid.

3.
   a. Will and Sid are friends.
   b. Will hid Sid.
   c. Sid gives a pill to Will.

H.   Write the word that goes with each picture.

1. _____   3. _____

2. _____

I.   How are you doing?

In this section you answered 56
questions. Count the number of
questions you got wrong and look
at the chart to see how you did.

NUMBER WRONG
  0—5   Excellent
  6—10   Great
11—15   Very Good
16—20   Good
21—25   OK

DIRECTIONS: When the student is comfortable with this format, similar exercises in later lessons can be assigned for independent work.
The answer key is on page 77.

★ The Family of Man ★

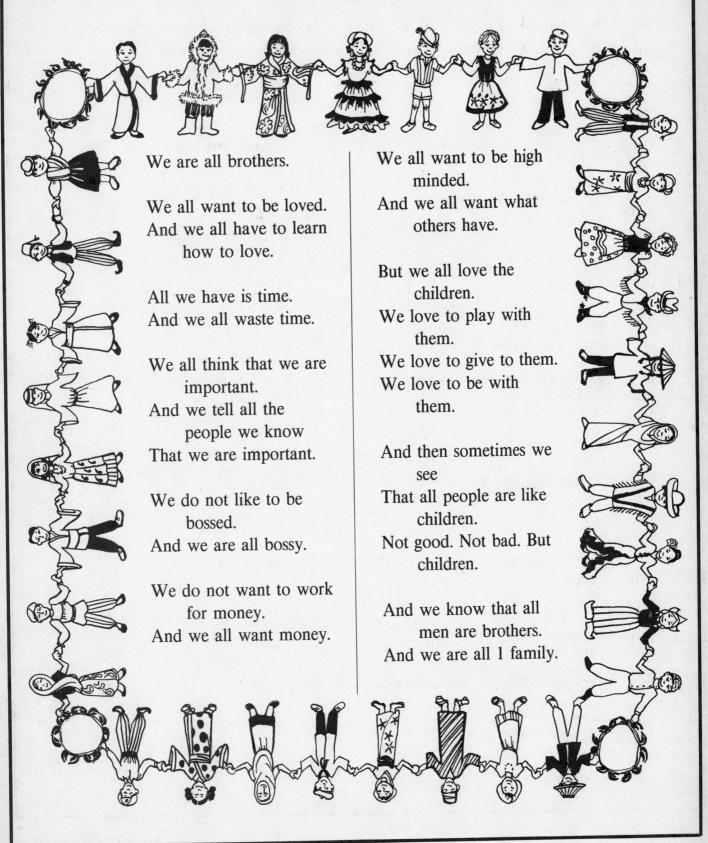

We are all brothers.

We all want to be loved.
And we all have to learn
how to love.

All we have is time.
And we all waste time.

We all think that we are
important.
And we tell all the
people we know
That we are important.

We do not like to be
bossed.
And we are all bossy.

We do not want to work
for money.
And we all want money.

We all want to be high
minded.
And we all want what
others have.

But we all love the
children.
We love to play with
them.
We love to give to them.
We love to be with
them.

And then sometimes we
see
That all people are like
children.
Not good. Not bad. But
children.

And we know that all
men are brothers.
And we are all 1 family.

DIRECTIONS: This section provides reinforcement of the vocabulary and skills presented in this lesson.

ON YOUR OWN

★ Playing with Words ★

1. Read the sentences. Then reread the words in bold print. Find the words in bold print in the box of letters. Words go from left to right and top to bottom.

```
x  g  w  a  y
c  o  m  e  b
j  o  r  z  i
k  d  w  h  o
m  o  r  e  f
```

a. I want **more** money.
b. Matt is a **good** man.
c. Are you going my **way**?
d. I want you to **come** with me.
e. They are 4 **of** my friends.
f. **Who** is she?
g. Are the boys **or** the girls going?

2. Unscramble the following sentences.

Example:
   friend good a I have.   I have a good friend.

a. a boy bad is He.   He _____

b. is teacher a Pam.   Pam _____

c. child Sal a not is.   Sal _____

d. likes cat My play to.   My _____

e. going Is she?   Is _____

3. Write your own tongue twister. Use the following words and any others you need.

school   see   she   some   sat   sag   Sal
sad   spend   sack   sup   Sam   Sid

Example: Sam, Sal, and Sid sat in school.

_____

_____

12

DIRECTIONS: After explaining these exercises to the student, assign them as independent work. The answer key is on page 77.

— ON YOUR OWN —

★ Thinking with Words ★

1. Decide which word or picture should go in the _____. Then circle it or write it.

   a. is to

      as

       is to _____

   b. **Good** is to **bad**

      as

      come is to _____.

      go   jam

2. What do you think? Spend some time thinking about your answer before you circle it.

   a. It is OK to hit children.   Yes   No   Maybe
   b. It is OK for children to play in school.   Yes   No   Maybe
   c. It is OK for teachers to hit children.   Yes   No   Maybe

3. Put an X on the word that does not belong in the column.

a.	b.	c.	d.
love	then	rat	school
like	learn	you	house
mill	teach	bat	good
	play	cat	

4. Who do you think wrote these sentences? Read the first sentence. Then guess who wrote it. Circle your answer. Spend some time thinking about why you circled one and not another. Do the other sentences in the same way.

   a. I like to play with my cats.   a boy   a man   cannot tell
   b. I want to nap.   an old man   a boy   cannot tell
   c. I like to read.   a teacher   a man   cannot tell

DIRECTIONS: Read the directions for each section. Exercise 1 covers analogies, item sets that are similar in some way. Exercise 3 concerns classification; the student should establish a relationship between the items, then eliminate the unrelated item. In exercises 2 and 4 the student makes inferences about his or her reading. Examples for each of these exercises might be helpful to the student. As the student becomes comfortable with these exercises, they can be assigned as independent work. The answer key for exercises 1 and 3 is on page 77.

ON YOUR OWN

★ If . . . ★

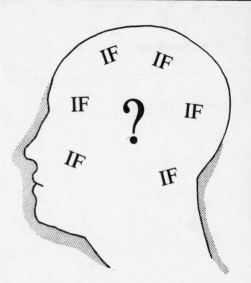

My mind is filled with "If's . . . . "

If I had money . . . . If I had time . . . .
If I had loved . . . . If I had worked at work . . . .
If I had not yelled . . . .
If I had played . . . . If I had yelled . . . .
If I had not married . . . . If I had children . . . .
IF . . . IF . . . IF . . .

My mind is filled with too many "If's . . . . "

★ Teaching or Nagging? ★

Al is Matt's dad. Matt was in high school in the 1940s. They are having a talk in 1944.

Matt: Dad, you always yell at me.

Al: I am not yelling at you. I want to tell you about the things I think are important.

Matt: Like how I spend my time?

Al: Sometimes I think you waste time. We have money. You do not have to work. Do your best at school. Make all A's.

Matt: But, Dad, I do OK at school. The teachers tell you that I am OK.

Al: The teachers tell me that you are like the other boys. They do not think about how things will be for you when you are old. I am your father. I am telling you to spend time with the books.

Matt: I like music. I like to do things with friends.

Al: You think about girls all the time. Spend a little time doing schoolwork.

Matt: Dad, do not nag.

Al: I am not nagging. I am telling you to learn all you can. People do not give you things when you are 35.

Matt: OK. OK. But when I have children, I will not be bossy with them.

Al: When you are old, you will think like me.

Two Reading Exercises: These exercises provide reinforcement and can be assigned as independent work.

The time is 1983. Ann is the child of Matt. She is in high school.

Matt: I think you have to spend time playing.

Ann: I am too old to play, Dad.

Matt: Then, do things with friends.

Ann: But I like to read.

Matt: How about music? You used to like to play music with friends.

Ann: Yes. I used to like music. But I want to make all A's in schoolwork.

Matt: You are good looking. All the boys will be jealous of the boy you go with.

Ann: All boys talk about is how important they are.

Matt: Being quiet is OK. But you have to have friends.

Ann: Dad, do not nag.

Matt: Did you tell me not to nag?

Ann: You look mad.

Matt: No. I am not mad. I am thinking. I used to think my Dad was a nag.

Ann: Was he?

Matt: No. I see that he loved me. He wanted the best for me.

Ann: Was he always telling you to make friends?

Matt: No. He wanted me to spend most of my time doing schoolwork.

Ann: Like I do?

Matt: Yes. I will not be bossy with you. I see that I cannot teach you the things important to me. You can see who I am and the things that I do. You have to learn the things that are important to you.

Does Matt talk to Ann like Al talked to him?

WOODROW WILSON

————————— • **Things to Think About When You Read Lesson 2** • —————————

NEW WORDS

1. president

    How many **presidents** have we had?
    What does the **president** do?

2. was   were

    How old **was** the 28th president when he learned to read?
    How old **were** you when you learned to read?

3. world

    What did the people of the **world** think of Woodrow Wilson?
    What do you think of Woodrow Wilson?

4. made

    Do you think Woodrow Wilson **made** many friends for the U.S.A?
    How do you think he **made** friends for the U.S.A?

5. war

    What **war** did the U.S.A. fight in 1917?
    What **war** did the U.S.A. fight in the 1960s and 1970s?

6. went

    When the U.S.A. **went** to war in 1917, did most of the people want war?
    When the U.S.A. **went** to war in the 1960s, did most of the people
       want war?

7. from

    What did Woodrow Wilson learn **from** his father?
    What do you want to learn **from** reading about Woodrow Wilson?

NEW WORDS: The instructor reads the new word and the first sentence of each pair. The student reads the second sentence of each pair.

From 1788 to 1985, the people of the U.S.A. had 40 presidents. Woodrow Wilson was the 28th president of the U.S.A. He learned to read when he was 11.

When he was a boy, Woodrow Wilson did not like school. His dad was his best friend. He was his best teacher, too. Woodrow Wilson learned many things from his dad. He learned to work for what was important.

At 29, Woodrow was a teacher. At 46, he was made president of Princeton University. Then at 56, he was made president of the U.S.A.

As president, Wilson worked for the working man. He wanted all the people of the world to be free. He did many things to make all people free.

From 1912 to 1916 Wilson did not want the U.S.A. to go to war. But in 1917, most of the people wanted to go to war. Wilson wanted the U.S.A. to go to war, too. And the U.S.A. went to war.

Wilson was a good president in the war. But he did not want another war. He did not want the children to see another war.

The people of the world loved Wilson. But the people of the U.S.A. did not. They did not want to think about war. They did not want to think about other people. They were mad at Wilson. They did not make Woodrow Wilson president in 1920.

Woodrow Wilson was president from 1912 to 1920. Woodrow Wilson was 1 of the best presidents the U.S.A. has had.

READING SELECTION: The student reads the passage with instructor assistance, if necessary.

A. Write your own title for the story.

_____

B. From the story, decide if the statements are true. Circle **Yes** or **No**.

1. Woodrow Wilson always liked school.   Yes   No
2. Woodrow Wilson liked war.   Yes   No
3. The people of the world loved Woodrow Wilson.   Yes   No
4. Woodrow Wilson learned to read when he was six.   Yes   No

C. What do you think?   Circle One

1. Woodrow Wilson was a good president.   Yes   No   Maybe
2. Woodrow Wilson had a good mind.   Yes   No   Maybe
3. Woodrow Wilson loved children.   Yes   No   Maybe

D. Write what you think.

1. I think Woodrow Wilson_____

_____

2. To be president _____

_____

> **Good readers** sometimes read a story 2 or 3 times in order to answer questions correctly.

E. Put the number 1, 2, or 3 next to each sentence to show what happened 1st, 2nd, and 3rd.

____ Woodrow Wilson was president of Princeton University.
____ Woodrow Wilson learned to read.
____ Woodrow Wilson was president of the U.S.A.

QUIZ: If necessary, assist the student with exercises A and D. When the student is comfortable with this exercise, similar exercises in later lessons can be assigned as independent work. The answer key is on page 77.

Learning to read is very much like learning any other skill. When you are learning to drive a car, you have to think about all the things you have to do to control the car. In the same way, it is important for you to know all the things you have to do to become a good reader.

Just as the goal of learning to drive is to make you into a driver who can act automatically without thinking about every little step, the goal of reading instruction is to make you into an ''automatic reader.'' When you get to the point when you know some words without having to figure them out, you will be on your way to becoming a good ''automatic reader.''

Remember, once you know a word, just say it. Once you can guess what a word is from the other words in the sentence, just say it. When you can read a word automatically, don't worry about all the other steps.

————— • **Skill Building** • —————

Good readers use the story to help them read words they do not know.

A. Think of a word to complete the sentence. Then write it.

We can learn many things from looking back into the 1900s.

We can _____ about the world.

We _____ learn about the U.S.A.

B. Each of these words is a combination of 2 words. Circle each of the 2 words inside the big one.

1. outcome   2. madman   3. madhouse

C. Add a letter to the word you already know. Say and write the new word.

all   NEW WORD

c + all = _____

f + all = _____

TIPS: Read these tips to the student and discuss them with him or her.
SKILL BUILDING: Read the lettered instructions to the student. The answer key is on page 77.

(19)

Good readers use a word's shape to help them remember the word.

D. Put each word in the shape that fits it.

from

was

E. Read each sentence and write the word that completes it.

president   was   world   made   war   went   from

1. I m _ _ _ him go to school.

2. He w _ _ my friend.

3. Do you want to be pr _ _ _ _ _ _ _?

4. The quiet girl w _ _ _ to work.

5. We will go fr _ _ her house to his house.

6. The w _ _ _ _ is big.

7. Do you want the U.S.A. to go to w _ _?

F. To learn the **er** ending write the correct word.

1. Pat is old.

   But Dan is _____.
                old older

2. Does the president like

   to _____?
      teach teacher

3. She is little.

   But I think that I am _____.
                          little littler

4. Will your baby be

   _____ for me?
   quiet quieter

G. Read the sentences. Then write the words that are in **bold print**.

I do not **mind** your **yelling**. I do not mind your nagging.
I do not mind your being jealous. I **do** mind your spending all the money.

m_____   y_____   d_____

DIRECTIONS: Exercise F shows how **er** can be added to a word to compare two things.
ADDITIONAL REINFORCEMENT: When the student is comfortable with the new words in this lesson, the flash cards at the end of the book can be used for reinforcement.

Manny writes:

That Woodrow Wilson was something. I think that he was a good teacher. Maybe he was a good president too.

But how did he go from being a teacher to being president? Little kids may think about being president. But not as they become older.

Does a man become president for the money? Or maybe he wants to be the most important man in the U.S.A? As for me, I do not want to be president of the U.S.A. I do not want to work all the time.

But does the president have to work all of the time? Maybe he does. Maybe he does not. Many people work for the president. He can tell other people what to do. He can work if he wants to work. But he does not have to work.

I am good at telling other people what to do. The people at work say I am a good boss. Sometimes my kids say that I am a nag. But they do what I tell them.

The more I think about it, the more I want to be president. Maybe I will be president at some time.

WHAT DO YOU THINK?

Do you think the president works all the time?

Do you want to be president?

READING TO KNOW OTHERS: This exercise can be assigned for independent work.
REMINDER: Flash cards for the new words are located at the end of the book and can be used at the instructor's discretion.

21

Look at the sample time line on the left and then fill in your own on the right.

1985	I go back to school.	1985 _____
	I have a baby.	_____
1980		1980 _____
	I am married.	_____
		_____
		_____
	I go to work.	_____
1970		1970 _____
Vietnam War		_____
		_____
		_____
1960		1960 _____
	I have a baby brother.	_____
		_____
Korean War	I go to school.	_____
1950		1950 _____
	I am a baby.	_____
World War 2	My Dad goes to war.	_____
1940		1940 _____
		_____
The Depression 1930		1930 _____
	My Dad goes to school.	_____
1920	My Dad is a baby.	1920 _____

DIRECTIONS: Read the instructions to the students. Encourage the students to fill in their own time lines, but assist them with spelling any words that they need help with. Reassure any student who has difficulty with the exercise that copying the model word for word is quite appropriate.

ĭ =

A.   Circle the picture of all words that make the **ĭ** sound.

ĭ

ĭ    **6**

B.   Fill in the blank to spell the word.

1.   p __ ll   3.   d __ g

2.   h __ p

C.   Read words with the **ĭ** sound in sentences.

1.   **I will** do **it**.   2.   She **is sick**.

D.   Use the words with the **ĭ** sound in sentences.

1.   Are you _____?
              it sick

2.   I see _____.
           it sick

E.   Circle the words that make the **ĭ** sound.

fight   with   mind   little   like   give

SOUNDING IT OUT: Read the instructions for each section to the student. The answer key for exercises B through H is on page 78.

㉓

F. Read the following sounds and words.

ib		im	
ĭ	bib	ĭ	dim
ĭ	fib	ĭ	him
ĭ	jib	ĭ	Jim
ĭ	rib	ĭ	Kim
		ĭ	rim
		ĭ	Tim
		ĭ	vim

1. Think of a sentence for each of the above words. Then say it.

2. Use the words above to fill in the blanks.

   a. Use a b __ __ with the baby.

   b. Give h __ __ a kiss.

   c. T __ __ and K __ __ are friends.

   d. Do not tell me a f __ __.

3. Spell the words on the lines below as they are said to you.

ib	im
a. _____	a. _____
b. _____	b. _____
c. _____	c. _____
d. _____	d. _____
e. _____	e. _____

NUMBER 3: Choose the words from each list in Section F.

G.   Circle the sentence that describes the picture.

1.
a.   Jim fibs to Tim.
b.   Jim and Tim are friends.
c.   Jim and Tim fight.

2.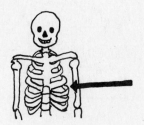
a.   Kim likes him.
b.   Kim has a bib for the baby.
c.   Kim likes Tim.

3.
a.   You can see a hill.
b.   You can see the rib.
c.   You can see a rim.

H.   Write the word that goes with each picture.

1. _____   2. _____

I.   How are you doing?

In this section you answered 45
questions. Count the number of
questions you got wrong and look
at the chart to see how you did.

NUMBER WRONG
 0—4   Excellent
 5—8   Great
 9—12 Very Good
13—16 Good
17—20 OK

ON YOUR OWN

★ Know Your Presidents ★

All of the presidents were important. They said and did important things. But they were people too. In many ways they were like you and me. They had families. They worked. They had friends. And sometimes they did not have all the things that they wanted.

Read about 3 presidents and the things they did. Read about who they were as people.

George Washington
President from 1789 to 1797

George Washington was married to Martha Washington. But they did not have children. He liked being president. But he did not love being president.

We will be a free people.

Abraham Lincoln
President from 1861 to 1865

Abraham Lincoln was married and had 4 boys. 1 of the boys was killed in the war. Mrs. Lincoln was always jealous. But when her boy was killed, she went mad.

All people will be free.

Franklin Roosevelt
President from 1933 to 1945

Franklin Roosevelt's family had money. But Franklin was sickly as a child. And he was sickly when he was president.

Children, people with no money, old people, workers without work, all are important.

DIRECTIONS: This page reinforces the skills and vocabulary words presented in this lesson. When the student is familiar with this format, these exercises can be assigned for independent work.

★ Playing with Words ★

1. Read the sentences. Then reread the words in bold print. Find the words in bold print in the box of letters. Words go from left to right and top to bottom.

p	x	q	w	b	g
r	z	q	e	c	h
e	w	o	r	l	d
s	a	g	e	u	v
i	s	f	r	o	m
d	h	j	k	w	x
e	m	a	d	e	y
n	q	b	c	n	z
t	w	a	r	t	c

a. I **made** him go.
b. He **was** my friend.
c. She is **president**.
d. The girl **went** to work.
e. We will go **from** her house.
f. The **world** is big.
g. Do you want to go to **war**?

2. Unscramble the following sentences.

Example:
have wants to Dan ham.   Dan <u>wants to have ham</u>.

a. loves Pam Tim.   Tim _____

b. lab They in learn the.   They learn _____

c. Kim best my is friend.   Kim _____

d. Married people more money need.   Married people _____

e. read to Sam them will.   Sam will _____

3. Write your own tongue twister. Use the following words and any others you need.

music   me   most   money   married   May
make   man   many   Mat   mind   my   men   mad
mop   map   mass   more   mill   made

Example: <u>Many married men make more money</u>.

_____

_____

DIRECTIONS: After explaining these exercises to the student, assign them as independent work. The answer key is on page 78.

ON YOUR OWN

★ Thinking with Words ★

1. Decide which word or picture should go in the _____. Then circle it or write it.

a.  is to

as

 is to _____

b. **Play** is to **boy**

as

work is to _____.

man   like

2. What do you think? Spend some time thinking about your answer before you circle it.

   a. Fighting is always bad.   Yes   No   Maybe

   b. War is always bad.   Yes   No   Maybe

   c. Killing is always bad.   Yes   No   Maybe

3. Put an X on the word that does not belong in the column.

a. Jan	b. old	c. Dad	d. at
Jack	little	Mother	or
use	bossy	more	do
Pam	fat	child	housework
Sid	when	brother	to

4. Who do you think wrote these sentences? Read the first sentence. Then guess who wrote it. Circle your answer. Spend some time thinking about why you circled one and not another. Do the other sentences in the same way.

   a. I love to talk.   a man   a woman   cannot tell

   b. I love to spend money.   a man   a woman   cannot tell

   c. I like to fight.   a little boy   an old man   cannot tell

DIRECTIONS: Read the directions for each section. Exercise 1 covers analogies, item sets that are similar in some way. Exercise 3 concerns classification; the student should establish a relationship between the items, then eliminate the unrelated item. In exercises 2 and 4 the student makes inferences about his or her reading. Examples for each of these exercises might be helpful to the student. As the student becomes comfortable with these exercises, they can be assigned as independent work. The answer key for exercises 1 and 3 is on page 78.

28

ON YOUR OWN

★ How to Tell When Your Child Is Jealous of Your Baby ★

People do not think that little children are jealous. But many children are jealous of babies.

It is important to know if your child is jealous. Then you can do something about it. Look for 3 things to see if your child is jealous.

A child may think that he has to be like a baby to be loved. He may talk baby talk. He may ask for a bib. If he does baby-like things, he is telling you something. He thinks you want the baby, not him.

Sometimes a child will be mad at the baby. He thinks the baby is too important to you. He thinks, "They have the baby. They do not want me." The child may ask you to give the baby away. If he tells you that he does not like the baby, he is telling you something. He thinks you want the baby, not him.

The little child who thinks that you do not love him may be sad. He may be quiet. He may not play the way he used to play. The child who always looks sad is telling you something, too. He thinks that you want the baby, not him.

If you think your child is jealous, read "How to Free Your Child from Being Jealous."

★ How to Free Your Child from Being Jealous ★

Many times a little child will be jealous of a baby. Your child becomes jealous when he thinks that you do not love him.

With a baby in the house, you have many things to do. You may not have time for your child. When you do not have time for him, he thinks he is not important. He thinks he is not wanted.

You may have made the child jealous with the things you did. You can free the child from being jealous.

You have to tell the child that you love him. You have to tell him that he is important. But children learn best from the things you do. You will have to make him see your love. You will have to play with him. You will have to read to him. You will have to be with him.

With 2 children in the house, you may think that you cannot make time. But you have to make the time to love the 2 of them.

TWO READING EXERCISES: These exercises provide reinforcement and can be assigned as independent work.

BOOKS TO TALK ABOUT

——— • **Things to Think About When You Read Lesson 3** • ———

NEW WORDS

1.	book	What things can **books** teach? Can **books** teach people how to read?
2.	on	Is "**On** Learning to Read" a good book? What is "**On** Learning to Read" about?
3.	write	When did Bruno Bettelheim **write** his book? When did Rudolf Flesch **write** his book?
4.	say	What does Bruno Bettelheim **say** about learning to read? What does Rudolf Flesch **say** about learning to read?
5.	story stories	Why does Bruno Bettelheim say reading **stories** is important? What does Rudolf Flesch think about **stories**?
6.	believe	Do you **believe** Bruno Bettelheim? Do you **believe** Rudolf Flesch?
7.	why	**Why** do people write books? **Why** do people read books?

NEW WORDS: The instructor reads the new word and the first sentence of each pair. The student reads the second sentence of each pair.

People write books about many things. But 2 books have said something about how people learn to read. The books say something about why people do not learn, too. Bruno Bettelheim wrote ''On Learning to Read'' in 1981. Rudolf Flesch wrote ''Why Johnny Can't Read'' in 1955.

''ON LEARNING TO READ''

Bruno Bettelheim wanted to know why some children became good readers. He wanted to know why other children were not good readers. He went to many schools. He looked at how children read. He looked at why children read.

He looked at the school books and story books. Some of the children did not like the books. They did not think that the books were important. They did not spend time reading. They did not become good readers.

Other children liked the reading books. They did spend time reading. They learned to read quickly. They were the good readers.

In his book, Bruno Bettelheim talks about the schools. He talks about the books. He wants the schools to use good books. He says that you have to spend time reading books to become a good reader.

''WHY JOHNNY CAN'T READ''

Rudolf Flesch thinks and talks about reading in another way. Flesch does not believe that children have to like books. He does not believe that books and stories have to be important.

To learn to read, Flesch thinks you have to know how to use **a, e, i, o,** and **u**.

A.   Write your own title for the story.

_____

B.   From the story, decide if the statements are true. Circle **Yes** or **No**.

1.   Bruno Bettelheim wrote a book on learning to read.   Yes   No

2.   Rudolf Flesch wrote a book on how to make money.   Yes   No

3.   Bruno Bettelheim and Rudolf Flesch think alike.   Yes   No

C.   What do you think?   Circle One

1.   Knowing and using **a, e, i, o,** and **u** is important
     for learning how to read.   Yes   No   Maybe

2.   Spending time reading is important to learn how to read.   Yes   No   Maybe

3.   It is good for teachers to read books on how to teach
     reading.   Yes   No   Maybe

D.   Write what you think.

1.   For me the best way of learning to read is _____

_____

2.   Reading about books on how to teach reading is _____

_____

QUIZ: If necessary, assist the student with exercises A and D. When the student is comfortable with this exercise, similar exercises in later lessons can be assigned as independent work. The answer key is on page 78.

When you see a word that you don't know, look at it to see if there is any part of it that you do know. Next, try to put the part you do know together with the rest of the word. You have had a lot of practice doing this in earlier lessons (**m** + **at** = mat, etc.).

Using parts of words does not always work, but it is still a good way to look at unknown words. Exercise C in ''Skill Building'' will give you practice in putting word parts together.

• Skill Building •

A.   Think of a word to complete the sentence. Then write it.

People write books about many things.
Some people write about work.

Some _____ write about the things they like to do.

_____ people write school books.

> **Good readers** know how to break long words into smaller parts.

B.   Each of these words is a combination of 2 words. Circle each of the 2 words inside the big one.

  1. kidnap   2. backpack   3. catnap

> **Good readers** use the words they do know to figure out the words they do not know.

C.   Add a letter to the word you already know. Say and write the new word.

all	NEW WORD	**all**	NEW WORD
h + all = _____		c + all = _____	
m + all = _____		t + all = _____	

TIPS: Read these tips to the student and discuss them with him or her.
SKILL BUILDING: Read the lettered instructions to the student. The answer key is on page 78.

(33)

D. Put each word in the shape that fits it.

why

write

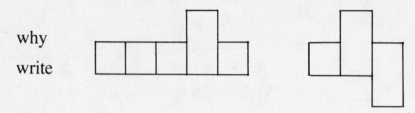

E. Read each sentence and write the word that completes it.

book   on   story   believe   write   say   why

1. He likes to s __ __ he is important.

2. I will wr __ __ __ to her when I have time.

3. I want to read the b __ __ __ .

4. Wh __ is he being bad?

5. Many people b __ __ __ __ __ __ the family is important.

6. Will he go o __ with the work?

7. I will tell you a good st __ __ __ .

F. To learn the **er** ending, write the correct word.

1. He likes to write books for children.

   He is a _____ .
   write writer

2. She wants to become a _____ .
   teach teacher

3. Why are some stories _____ ?
   sad sadder

4. This house is high.

   But the school is _____ .
   high higher

G. Read the sentences. Then write the words that are in **bold print**.

We have 2 **little** children. Pam is the **baby**.
She is a good baby. Tim is 3. He is good, too.

l_____   b_____

DIRECTIONS: Exercise F shows how **er** can be added to a word to show "one who does something" or a doer. **Er** can also be used to compare two things.

ADDITIONAL REINFORCEMENT: When the student is comfortable with the new words in this lesson, the flash cards at the end of the book can be used for reinforcement.

(34)

Mike writes:

I want to know about many, many things. I want to know how we think. And why we think the way we do. And why we think about some things but not other things.

I want to know how children learn to talk. How do little babies learn? What makes them want to learn?

And I want to learn all I can about reading. What goes on in the reader's mind when he reads? What does reading have to do with thinking? What does reading have to do with talking?

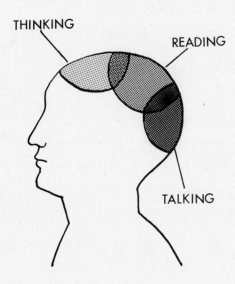

This is the way I think
things work.

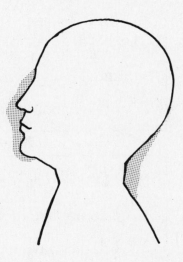

How do you think
things work?

READING TO KNOW OTHERS: This exercise can be assigned for independent work.
REMINDER: Flash cards for the new words are located at the end of the book and can be used at the instructor's discretion.

35

Read the reasons that other people have given for improving or not improving their writing. Then decide if you want to improve your writing or not, and list the reasons.

Why I want to become good at writing:

1. When I work to 9 p.m. I do not see my kids. I want to write to them.

2. I want to become a boss at work. And bosses have to know how to write.

3. I think good writers become good readers.

Why I do not want to work on my writing:

1. I do not like to write.

2. I do not have to write at work.

3. I do not have to write to my family.

_____

_____

_____

_____

_____

_____

DIRECTIONS: Read the instructions to the students. Encourage the students to write their own lists of reasons for wanting to improve their writing, but assist them with spelling any words they need help with. Reassure any student who has difficulty with the exercise that copying the model word for word is quite appropriate. If the student hesitates to write, the student should dictate his or her list to the instructor. The instructor should write the list on a separate piece of paper and then let the student copy it into the book.

ĭ =

A. Circle the picture of all words that make the **ĭ** sound.

ĭ

ĭ

B. Fill in the blank to spell the word.

1. p __ g    3. b __ b

2. m __ tt

C. Read words with the **ĭ** sound in sentences.

1. **Give him** a **tip**.   2. **Did** she **kiss** you?

D. Use the words with the **ĭ** sound in sentences.

1. I want to _____ my child.
        tip kiss

2. The _____ was $3.00.
        tip kiss

E. Circle the words that make the **ĭ** sound.

with   fight   will   child   important   like

SOUNDING IT OUT: Read the instructions for each section to the student. The answer key for exercises B through I is on page 78.

37

F.   Read the following sounds and words.

	ick		**it**
ĭ	Dick	ĭ	bit
ĭ	kick	ĭ	fit
ĭ	lick	ĭ	hit
ĭ	Mick	ĭ	kit
ĭ	Nick	ĭ	lit
ĭ	pick	ĭ	pit
ĭ	quick	ĭ	quit
ĭ	Rick	ĭ	sit
ĭ	sick	ĭ	wit

1.   Think of a sentence for each of the above words. Then say it.

2.   Use the words above to fill in the blanks.

a.   He will p _ _ _ the girl he wants to see.

b.   I am s _ _ _ of her.

c.   He h _ _ the cat.

d.   Then the cat b _ _ him.

e.   Are you going to see R _ _ _?

f.   Will you s _ _ with me?

3.   Spell the words on the lines below as they are said to you.

	ick		**it**
a.	_____	a.	_____
b.	_____	b.	_____
c.	_____	c.	_____
d.	_____	d.	_____
e.	_____	e.	_____

G.   Remember the sound ă makes. Read the following sentences.

1.   Pat and Hal are married.   2.   Jack sat on the back of the mat.

NUMBER 3: Choose the words from each list in Section F.

H. Circle the sentence that describes the picture.

1.
   a. Nick quit work.
   b. Nick kicks.
   c. Dick is quick.

2.
   a. Mick sits.
   b. Mick is sick.
   c. Mick likes Jill.

3.
   a. Rick bit the pit.
   b. Rick is sick.
   c. Rick looks fit.

I. Write the word that goes with each picture.

1. _Kick_ 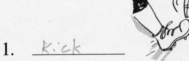   3. _hit_

2. _pit_

J. How are you doing?

In this section you answered 57 questions. Count the number of questions you got wrong and look at the chart to see how you did.

NUMBER WRONG
0—5   Excellent
6—10   Great
11—15 Very Good
16—21 Good
22—27 OK

DIRECTIONS: When the student is comfortable with this format, similar exercises in later lessons can be assigned for independent work. The answer key is on page 78.
ADDITIONAL REINFORCEMENT: The Advanced Phonics Exercises on pages 75 and 76 can be used with those students who completed Sounding It Out without difficulty.

ON YOUR OWN

★ Writing Without Reading ★

Can a man write books if he is not good at reading? Some people have. If you want, you can do it, too.

You can tell the story to a friend. Then have him write it for you. But what if you do not have a friend to write for you? Maybe you do not want a friend to write for you.

If you want to write a book, think about using a tape recorder. With a tape recorder you can write a book. Many people who are good at reading use a tape recorder. They do not have time to write. They talk into the tape recorder. Then they have other people write what they have said.

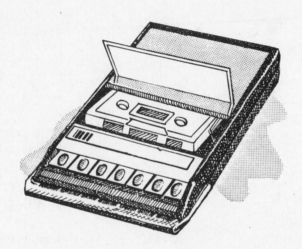

TAPE RECORDER

★ What to Write About ★

When you write a book. what do you write about? Write about something you know about. You may want to write about your work. Maybe you want to write about the things that you do in your free time. Maybe you can write a book about your family or friends. Write a book about children or for children.

Most times you will not know **all** the things that you are writing on. It will be important for you to learn all you can. You can talk to people. You can read about what you are writing on.

You may not make any money writing a book. But you will learn many things. And maybe you will have a good time writing your book!

TWO READING EXERCISES: These exercises provide reinforcement and can be assigned as independent work.

1. Read the sentences. Then reread the words in bold print. Find the words in bold print in the box of letters. Words go from left to right and top to bottom.

c	s	a	y	j	m	n
d	t	w	h	y	p	q
b	o	o	k	v	c	f
f	r	n	w	x	z	d
g	y	w	r	i	t	e
b	e	l	i	e	v	e

a. What did Pam **say**?

b. I will **write** to her.

c. I want to read the **book**.

d. **Why** is he going?

e. Many people **believe** in you.

f. Will he go **on** to work?

g. I will tell you a **story**.

2. Unscramble the following sentences.

Example:

school at She sick was.   She <u>was sick at school</u>.

a. talk Nick about school Dan and.   Dan and _____

b. looks Jill her map at.   Jill _____

c. president to be wants Pam.   Pam _____

d. I music want play to.   I _____

e. The hill on is a school.   The _____

3. Write your own tongue twister. Use the following words and any others you need.

time	think	to	thing	the	talk	they
tell	tan	then	tag	teach	teacher	
tax	them	tack	tap	tab	till	Tim

Example: <u>They tell time to the teachers, but Tim taps them</u>.

_____

_____

DIRECTIONS: After explaining these exercises to the student, assign them as independent work. The answer key is on page 78.

41

★ Thinking with Words ★

1. Decide which word should go in the _____. Then write it.

   a. **Play** is to **music**

      as

      read is to _____.
         book come

   b. **Me** is to **my**

      as

      you is to _____.
         hit your

2. What do you think? Spend some time thinking about your answer before you circle it.

   a. It is OK for married people to be jealous.   Yes   No   Maybe
   b. It is OK for married people to fight.   Yes   No   Maybe
   c. It is OK for married people to nag.   Yes   No   Maybe

3. Put an X on the word that does not belong in the column.

   a. kick   c. Mick   e. man
      fight   Sam   think
      friend   Dan   girl
      kill   learn   child

   b. kick   d. hat   f. is
      hit   she   are
      jab   her   them
      pan   him   was

4. Who do you think wrote these sentences? Read the first sentence. Then guess who wrote it. Circle your answer. Spend some time thinking about why you circled one and not another. Do the other sentences in the same way.

   a. I hit the van.   a child   a man   cannot tell
   b. Mind the teacher.   a man   a girl   cannot tell
   c. I have 2 children.   a boy   a man   cannot tell

DIRECTIONS: Read the directions for each section. Exercise 1 covers analogies, item sets that are similar in some way. Exercise 3 concerns classification; the student should establish a relationship between the items, then eliminate the unrelated item. In exercises 2 and 4 the student makes inferences about his or her reading. Examples for each of these exercises might be helpful to the student. As the student becomes comfortable with these exercises, they can be assigned as independent work. The answer key for exercises 1 and 3 is on page 78.

★ Work without Working ★

Pam is 18. She is in high school. She thinks about what she will do when she is 19. She wants to work. But she cannot think of anything that she can do.

Pam talks to her friends. Many of her friends are going to be married. They tell her not to think about work. They tell her, "You are good looking. You have a boyfriend. You will not have to work."

Pam thinks about being married. She likes her boyfriend. She likes children, and housework is OK. But she does not want to be married at 19. She wants to go places and see things.

Pam talks to her dad. He tells her not to think about money. She can go on in school.

Pam thinks school is OK. But she does not want more schooling.

Pam thinks about the things that she likes to do. She likes to talk to people. She likes to read. And she loves to write.

Pam wants to make money. But she does not think money is all-important. She thinks people are. She likes to do things for others.

Pam talks to some of her Dad's friends. They tell her to look into working with old people.

Pam does look into it. The money is not good, but Pam wants to do it.

From 9 a.m. to 5 p.m. Pam talks to old people, reads to them, and writes for them. Pam tells her friends that she works without working.

DIRECTIONS: This section provides reinforcement of the vocabulary and skills presented in this lesson. When the student is comfortable with the format of this section, these exercises in later lessons can be assigned for independent work.

43

THE BEST MINDS: ALBERT EINSTEIN

• Things to Think About When You Read Lesson 4 •

NEW WORDS

1. one
Most people think Einstein had **one** of the best minds.
Do you think he had **one** of the best minds?

2. that
How do we know **that** Einstein had a good mind?
Was he an important man?

3. live
Did Einstein **live** like an important man?
How did he **live**?

4. slow
What was Einstein **slow** at learning?
What was he quick at learning?

5. adult
When he was a child, did Einstein like school?
When he was an **adult**, did Einstein like school?

6. place
In how many **places** did Einstein teach?
In how many **places** did Einstein live?

7. any
Did Einstein have **any** children?
Did he have **any** friends?

NEW WORDS: The instructor reads the new word and the first sentence of each pair. The student reads the second sentence of each pair.

When Albert Einstein was a child, he learned some things slowly. He was not good at talking at 2, 3, 4, or 9! He learned to read when he was 9. Many people believe, slow or not, Albert Einstein had one of the best minds.

Albert Einstein was a child in the 1880s. He did not play with any other children. He liked to think about things. He liked to play music, too. He was good at playing music. But he was the best at thinking.

Einstein liked to think, but he did not like school. He did many things that made the teachers mad. At 16, he was kicked out of high school. He then went to another school. When he was an adult, he was a teacher. He was a teacher at 5 schools.

Einstein married 2 times. He had 2 children. He worked and lived in Princeton, New Jersey, from 1933 to 1955.

Albert Einstein was at his best when he was thinking about important things. He was not good at thinking about things like money or a place to live.

Albert Einstein believed in doing things for other people. He did not think that he was important. He did not want others to think that he was important. Important or not, he was good at thinking. His thinking has made many things the way they are.

READING SELECTION: The student reads the passage with instructor assistance, if necessary.

45

A. Write your own title for the story.

_____

> **Good readers** sometimes read a story 2 or 3 times in order to answer questions correctly.

B. From the story, decide if the statements are true. Circle **Yes** or **No**.

   1. Albert Einstein married 2 times.   Yes   No

   2. Albert Einstein had 3 children.   Yes   No

   3. Albert Einstein learned to read when he was 9.   Yes   No

   4. Albert Einstein wanted other people to think
       that he was important.   Yes   No

C. What do you think?   Circle One

   1. Albert Einstein had a good mind.   Yes   No   Maybe

   2. Albert Einstein was important.   Yes   No   Maybe

   3. You can be slow at reading and have a good mind.   Yes   No   Maybe

D. Write what you think.

   1. Albert Einstein was _____

      _____

   2. Having a good mind _____

      _____

E. Put the number 1, 2, or 3 next to each sentence to show what happened 1st, 2nd, and 3rd.

   ____ Albert Einstein worked in Princeton.

   ____ Albert Einstein was kicked out of high school.

   ____ Albert Einstein learned to talk.

QUIZ: If necessary, assist the student with exercises A and D. When the student is comfortable with this exercise, similar exercises in later lessons can be assigned as independent work. The answer key is on page 79.

(To be read to the student by the instructor)

One of the most important parts of learning to read is practice. If you have not been practicing your reading when you are away from school, making a schedule may help. You and I can discuss and then write down the times you find most convenient for reading. You may want to find time in your schedule *every* day for reading, or you may want to give yourself one day a week away from reading.

Remember, though, schedules look nice but they only work if you make them work. Once you have made up a schedule, do your best to stick to it.

———— • **Skill Building** • ————

A. Think of a word to complete the sentence. Then write it.

Most people are good at something.

Some people _____ good at writing books.

Some people are _____ at making money.

Some people are good _____ talking.

Most _____ are good at spending money.

B. Each of these words is a combination of 2 other words. Circle each of the 2 words inside the big one.

1. anything   2. anyway   3. anyhow

C. Add a letter to the word you already know. Say and write the new word.

war   NEW WORD

war + m = _____

war + p = _____

D. Put each word in the shape that fits it.

that
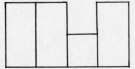
one

TIPS: Read these tips to the student and discuss them with him or her.
SKILL BUILDING: Read the lettered instructions to the student. The answer key is on page 79.

(47)

E. Read each sentence and write the word that completes it.

    any   adult   live   one   place   slow   that

    1. Do you have a pl __ __ __ to go?

    2. Most people are sl __ __ at learning something.

    3. I want to l __ __ __ in a big house.

    4. I will see th __ __ she goes to school.

    5. The children mind an a __ __ __ __ best.

    6. She has o __ __ baby.

    7. Will you see a __ __ of his friends?

    +--+
    | **Good readers** know word endings. |
    +--+

F. To learn the **ing**, **ly**, and **er** endings, write the correct word.

    1. I am _____ to her.   4. He _____.
            friend friendly   works worker

    2. He is a _____ boy.   5. Are you _____ a book?
            bad badly   write writing

    3. She is a good _____.   6. She is a _____ girl.
            read reader   quiet quietly

G. Read the sentences. Then write the words that are in **bold print**.

    He makes good **money**. He spends the money on his **house**.
    But he works all the time. He does not see the house.

    m_____   h_____

    +--+
    | **Good readers** know the different ways a word can be used. |
    +--+

H. Circle the word that is repeated each time you see it.

    He lives at 15 School Place.

    Tell me about the place.

    Place it in that hat.

DIRECTIONS: Exercise F reviews the endings that have been introduced in previous lessons.
ADDITIONAL REINFORCEMENT: When the student is comfortable with the new words in this lesson, the flash cards at the end of the book
can be used for reinforcement.

Sam writes:

Albert Einstein lived in Princeton. And I live in Princeton too. I did not know him. I was a kid in the 1950s.

But some of the old people tell stories about him. I will tell you 3 of the stories.

Story 1

Can I do something for you, Al?

I cannot think of what I wanted.

Story 2

Can I do something for you, Al?

I know what I want. But I do not have the money with me.

What is he writing about?

I do not know what he is writing. But it has to be important.

Story 3

What did he write?

✔ the story you liked most.

Story 1 _____

Story 2 _____

Story 3 _____

READING TO KNOW OTHERS: This exercise can be assigned for independent work.
REMINDER: Flash cards for the new words are located at the end of the book and can be used at the instructor's discretion.

(49)

Jack has used 3 categories to rate how he does things. Read what he has written. Then fill in your own 3 categories.

Things that I am good at:	Things that I do OK:	Things that I am not too good at:
talking to people	housework	reading books
playing with children	reading maps	writing at work
fixing things	telling stories	
spending money	working	
playing music	writing in school	
reading in school		

Things that I am good at:	Things that I do OK:	Things that I am not too good at:
_____	_____	_____
_____	_____	_____
_____	_____	_____
_____	_____	_____

DIRECTIONS: Read the instructions to the students. Encourage the students to write their own lists, but assist them with spelling any words that they need help with. Reassure any student who has difficulty with the exercise that copying the model word for word is quite appropriate. If the student hesitates to write, the student should dictate his or her list to the instructor. The instructor should write the list on a separate piece of paper and then let the student copy it into the book.

ĭ =

A.   Circle the picture of all words that make the **ĭ** sound.

ĭ

ĭ

B.   Fill in the blank to spell the word.

1.   h __ ll

2.   w __ g

3.   s __ p

C.   Read words with the **ĭ** sound in sentences.

1.   You **will win**.   2.   I **miss** you.

D.   Use words with the **ĭ** sound in sentences.

1.   I _____ you, too.   2.   I love to _____ .
     win miss   win miss

E.   Circle the words that make the **ĭ** or **ă** sound.

1.   ĭ   Bill   quiet   Sid   like   lip   high

2.   ă   fan   waste   make   hat   pack   way

SOUNDING IT OUT: Read the instructions for each section to the student. The answer key for exercises B through I is on page 79.

F.   Read the following sounds and words.

	in		**ig**
ĭ	bin	ĭ	big
ĭ	fin	ĭ	dig
ĭ	pin	ĭ	fig
ĭ	sin	ĭ	pig
ĭ	tin	ĭ	rig
ĭ	win	ĭ	wig

1.   Think of a sentence for each of the above words. Then say it.

2.   Use the words above to fill in the blanks.

   a.   Are you going to w __ __?

   b.   It is made of t __ __.

   c.   He is a b __ __ man.

   d.   Most people think killing is a s __ __.

   e.   He has 10 p __ __ s.

3.   Spell the words on the lines below as they are said to you.

in	**ig**
a. _____	a. _____
b. _____	b. _____
c. _____	c. _____
d. _____	d. _____
e. _____	e. _____

G.   Remember the sound **ă** makes. Read the following sentences.

1.   Pass the ham to Dan.
2.   My Dad will wax the cab.
3.   Sal is bad at reading maps.

NUMBER 3: Choose the words from each list in Section F.

H. Circle the sentence that describes the picture.

1.
   a. The pig has a bib.
   b. The pig digs.
   c. The pig is big.

2.
   a. Tim has a pin.
   b. Tim wins.
   c. Tim has a big rig.

3.
   a. Bill has a pin.
   b. Bill has a wig.
   c. Bill has a pig.

I. Write the word that goes with each picture.

1. _____   3. _____

2. _____

J. How are you doing?

In this section you answered 56 questions. Count the number of questions you got wrong and look at the chart to see how you did.

NUMBER WRONG	
0—5	Excellent
6—10	Great
11—15	Very Good
16—20	Good
21—25	OK

DIRECTIONS: When the student is comfortable with this format, similar exercises in later lessons can be assigned for independent work. The answer key is on page 79.

ADDITIONAL REINFORCEMENT: The Advanced Phonics Exercises on pages 75 and 76 can be used with those students who completed Sounding It Out without difficulty.

Little kids like to tell people, "He made me do it. She made me do it."

Adults do not tell people, "He made me do it. She made me do it." But adults think others make them do things.

Kids will tell each other, "I had to fight. He made me yell. With all the things he did to me, I had to hit him."

Adults tell children, "No one makes you do anything." Adults have to tell adults, "No one can make you think anything."

If you are jealous or sad, you want to be jealous or sad. No one can make you jealous or sad. Jealous and sad are all in your mind. And it is **your** mind.

People have to see the mind is a free place. You can be who you want to be. No one or no thing can make you be anything you do not want to be. It's your mind.

★ 4 Good Ways of Thinking ★

1. Know what you can do and what you cannot do. You cannot make a brother or friend come back from fighting in a war. You **can** write to them and tell them that you are thinking about them.

2. Do not waste time thinking about the things you cannot do anything about. You may feel bad when someone in your family is sick. But many times you cannot do anything about it. Do what you can do. Do not spend time thinking about all the things you cannot do.

3. Spend time thinking about the things you can do. If you want more friends, think about going out more. If you want to learn something, go to school. If you want more money, think about ways to make it.

4. Believe you can do the things you want to do. When you believe you can do things, other people will believe you can do things, too. If you want to become a boss at work, believe you can do the work. Others will believe you can do it, too. If you believe people will like you, they will. If you believe you can learn something, you will learn it.

TWO READING EXERCISES: These exercises provide reinforcement and can be assigned as independent work.

ON YOUR OWN

★ Playing with Words ★

1. Read the sentences. Then reread the words in bold print. Find the words in bold print in the box of letters. Words go from left to right and top to bottom.

```
b  p  t  h  a  t
s  l  o  w  f  g
j  a  n  y  k  m
q  c  e  u  w  x
r  e  l  i  v  e
a  d  u  l  t  z
```

a. Do you have a **place** to go?
b. Most people are **slow** at learning something.
c. I **live** in a big house.
d. I will see **that** she goes.
e. He is an **adult**.
f. She has **one** baby.
g. Will you see **any** friends?

2. Unscramble the following sentences.

Example:
   adult an is Jane.   Jane <u>is an adult</u>.

a. like music slow I.   I _____

b. Nan that mat made.   Nan _____

c. likes Pam place a quiet. Pam _____

d. Anyone president can be.   Anyone _____

e. wants work to Sid.   Sid _____

3. Write your own tongue twister. Use the following words and any others you need.

he   house   have   her   hat   high   how

Hal   had   him   hill   hid   hit

Example: <u>Hal hid her hat high on the hill</u>.

_____

_____

DIRECTIONS: After explaining these exercises to the student, assign them as independent work. The answer key is on page 79.

ON YOUR OWN

★ Thinking with Words ★

1. Decide which word should go in the _____. Then write it.

   a. **Adult** is to **baby**

      as

      big is to _____.

                    little fat

   b. **Slow** is to **quick**

      as

      in is to _____.

                  all out

2. What do you think? Spend some time thinking about your answer before you circle it.

   a. A dog can be a good friend.   Yes   No   Maybe

   b. It is important to have many friends.   Yes   No   Maybe

   c. It is good to have friends at work.   Yes   No   Maybe

3. Put an X on the word that does not belong in the column.

a. tag	c. president	e. book
tap	boss	say
tan	teacher	map
tax	feel	
children		

b. pig	d. come	f. mat
van	see	teach
dog	go	read
cat	wig	learn

4. Who do you think wrote these sentences? Read the first sentence. Then guess who wrote it. Circle your answer. Spend some time thinking about why you circled one and not another. Do the other sentences in the same way.

   a. I will be an adult.   a man   a girl   cannot tell

   b. I have a big family.   a boy   a man   cannot tell

   c. I do not want many children.   a boy   a girl   cannot tell

DIRECTIONS: Read the directions for each section. Exercise 1 covers analogies, item sets that are similar in some way. Exercise 3 concerns classification; the student should establish a relationship between the items, then eliminate the unrelated item. In exercises 2 and 4 the student makes inferences about his or her reading. Examples for each of these exercises might be helpful to the student. As the student becomes comfortable with these exercises, they can be assigned as independent work. The answer key for exercises 1 and 3 is on page 79.

56

Bill Win had money.
And he had schooling.
Bill Win was an important man.

Bill Win had a quick mind.
And he had a good family.
Bill Win was an important man.

Bill Win had friends.
And he had a big house.
Bill Win was an important man.

Bill Win wrote books.
And he did important work.
Bill Win was an important man.

Bill Win, the important man,
Had all the things that we wanted.

But then, Bill Win, that important man,
Went to his big house
And killed himself.

WHAT DO YOU THINK?

1. Do you think someone who has money, a big house, and a good family is important?

2. What makes someone important?

3. Can someone not have things and be important?

4. What do you think most people want? What do you want?

5. Do you think someone who has money can be sad?

6. What do you think most people live for?

DIRECTIONS: This section provides reinforcement of the vocabulary and skills presented in this lesson. When the student is comfortable with the format of this section, these exercises in later lessons can be assigned for independent work.

57

PEOPLE TELL WHY THEY DID NOT LEARN TO READ

• Things People Will Talk About in Lesson 5 •

NEW WORDS

1. woman   women
Most of my teachers were **women**.
I used to think reading was for girls and **women**.

2. feel
Reading used to make me **feel** sick.
I did not **feel** like doing schoolwork.

3. mother
My **mother** had 10 kids.
My **mother** did not have time for my schoolwork.

4. get
I used to **get** out of reading.
I used to **get** my friends to read to me.

5. ask
I said I was sick when the teacher **asked** me to read.
My teachers did not **ask** me to read.

6. afraid
I was **afraid** of the reading teacher.
I was **afraid** of school.

7. first
My **first** teacher did not like me.
I did not like my **first** teacher.

NEW WORDS: The instructor reads the new word and the first sentence of each pair. The student reads the second sentence of each pair.

Pat writes: When I was little, the schools did not have reading teachers. One teacher had 35 kids. The teachers did not have time for me. First of all, they wanted me to sit and be quiet. I sat and I was quiet. But I did not learn how to read.

Kim writes: When I was a little kid, we lived in 5 places. I went to 6 schools. Going to 6 schools was not good for me. The teachers did not get to know me. I did not get to know them.

Tim writes: I used to get out of reading. When the teacher asked me to read, I said I was sick. I said I was sick 7 or 8 times. Then the teacher did not ask me to read anymore.

Hal writes: When I was little, I did not want to read about Dick and his little cat. Most of my teachers were women. I used to think reading was for girls. I used to think reading was a waste. I did not want to learn. And I did not learn.

Jan writes: My mother and dad did not want me to go to school. They did not feel that reading was important. They did not feel that school was important. I worked with my dad from the time I was 8. I did not learn to read. But I learned other things.

Rick writes: When I was little, I did not like sitting in one place. I always had to be doing something. To learn to read, I had to sit. But I did not learn to read.

Sid writes: My mother and dad worked all the time. They had 10 children. They had to work for the family. They did not have time for my schoolwork. Some of my brothers did OK in school. Some of us did badly.

Sam writes: When I was in school, I was bad. I was always fighting. I kicked kids. I would yell. I made the teachers mad. Sometimes the teachers hit me. I was not afraid of them. But I did not want to learn anything from them.

Bill writes: My dad did not know how to read. People say I am like my dad. Maybe I wanted to be like him. Like him, I did not learn to read.

Al writes: I was afraid of the reading teacher. My teacher was not a woman. He was a big man. He made me do the work. I learned some things from him.

READING SELECTION: The student reads the passage with instructor assistance, if necessary.

Most people find some words harder to learn than other words. When you come across a word that is hard to learn, you just have to work harder to learn it.

We already talked about how you can write the word over and over as you say it. You can also put the word in a sentence as you look at it. Or you could study its shape.

Here is another way of learning a difficult word. Write your difficult word on a card. Then go through a newspaper or magazine looking for it. Keep looking back at your card and saying the word as you look for it. When you find the word, underline it. Or cut it out and tape it to the card.

There are many ways to learn difficult words. You may have some other ideas. Use the way that works best for you.

──────────── • **Skill Building** • ────────────

A. Think of a word to complete the sentence. Then write it.

I like to read.

I _____ to read books.

I like to _____ stories.

B. Each of these words is a combination of 2 other words. Circle each of the 2 words inside the big one.

1. anyone   2. catnip   3. into

C. Add a letter to the word you already know. Say and write the new word.

war   NEW WORD

war + n = _____

war + t = _____

D. Put each word in the shape that fits it.

get

feel

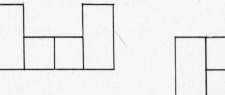

> **Good readers** make sure every sentence makes sense.

E. Read each sentence and write the word that completes it.

first   get   ask   feel   woman   afraid   mother

1. I know that w _ _ _ _ from work.

2. She is a good m _ _ _ _ _.

3. F _ _ _ _ we have to see her.

4. How do you f _ _ _?

5. Did you g _ _ the money?

6. I will a _ _ her to go.

7. Rick is a _ _ _ _ _ of cats.

F. To learn the **er**, **ly**, and **ing** endings, write the correct word.

1. This bus is _____.
    slow slowly

2. He is big.

    But I am _____.
    big bigger

3. She is _____.
    friend friendly

4. She is _____ old.
    get getting

5. I win all the time.

    I am a _____.
    win winner

> **Good readers** practice reading and writing the words they already know.

G. Read the sentences. Then write the words that are in **bold print**.

He is my **best** friend. He is a family man.
He is a teacher. He is my **brother**.

b_____   br_____

H. Circle the word that is repeated each time you see it.

Kim is a mother.

Do not mother me.

DIRECTIONS: Exercise F reviews the endings that have been introduced in previous lessons.
ADDITIONAL REINFORCEMENT: When the student is comfortable with the new words in this lesson, the flash cards at the end of the book can be used for reinforcement.

I know that many, many people are not too good at reading. I am one of them. But no one at work knows it. And I have not talked to my friends about it.

I work at a school fixing things. Most people tell me what they want me to do. But some of the teachers write to me. Then I go back to them. I tell them that I cannot read what they wrote. Most times I say, "Your writing is bad. No one can read it but you."

Most of my friends do not like to read. We do not talk about books or things like that. My best friend has a van. I like to work on it with him. Sometimes that is all we do. Other times we go places.

My mother knows that I am not a good reader. And my girlfriend knows too. When I have kids, I will not tell them that I cannot read some things. I will go to school and become a good reader.

Did you know that 1 out of 5 people cannot read this story?

READING TO KNOW OTHERS: This exercise can be assigned for independent work.
REMINDER: Flash cards for the new words are located at the end of the book and can be used at the instructor's discretion.

Read the first and second letters and Ann's answers. Then read the third letter and write an answer to it.

Letter to Ann

Ann,
  I have a girlfriend. We are going to be married. Do I have to tell her that I am not a good reader?

  A Boyfriend

Answer from Ann

Boyfriend,
  You have to talk to your girlfriend before you are married. What are you afraid of? She loves you, not the way you read.

  Ann

Letter to Ann

Ann,
  I have a little girl. She is six. I can read some stories to her, but not all of them.
  Do I have to tell her that I am not good at reading?

  A Dad

Answer from Ann

Dad,
  You do not **have to** tell your little girl. You can if you want to. But you do not **have to**.

  Ann

Letter to you

  I like the work that I do. And I am good at it. But I am not a good reader. And the boss does not know. Do I have to tell her?

  A Good Worker

Answer from you

Worker,

_____

_____

_____

_____

_____

DIRECTIONS: Read the instructions to the students. Encourage the students to write their own answers, but assist them with spelling any words that they need help with. Reassure any student who has difficulty with the exercise that copying the model word for word is quite appropriate. If the student hesitates to write, the student should dictate his or her answer to the instructor. The instructor should write the answer on a separate piece of paper and then let the student copy it into the book.

ă = 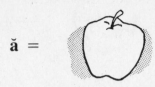   ĭ =

A.   Circle the picture of the word that begins with the **ĭ** or **ă** sound.

1. **ĭ**

2. **ă**

3. **ĭ**

4. **ă**

5. **ă**

B.   Fill in the blank with **ă** or **ĭ** to spell the word.

1. c __ t      3. l __ ps

2. p __ g      4. p __ n

C.   Circle the words that make the **ă** or **ĭ** sound.

1. **ă**   family   hand   ask   saw   way   war   farm   happen

2. **ĭ**   child   mind   first   fill   miss   pick   fight   pit

SOUNDING IT OUT: Read the instructions for each section to the student. The answer key for exercises B through G is on page 80.

D. Read the following sounds and words.

ip		**iss**		**ix**	
ĭ	dip	ĭ	kiss	ĭ	fix
ĭ	hip	ĭ	miss	ĭ	mix
ĭ	lip				
ĭ	rip				
ĭ	ship				
ĭ	sip				
ĭ	tip				

1. Think of a sentence for each of the above words. Then say it.

2. Use the words above to fill in the blanks.

   a. Did you k _ _ _ her?

   b. Can you f _ _ it?

   c. Give him a t _ _.

   d. Do not r _ _ it.

   e. I will m _ _ _ you.

3. Spell the words on the lines below as they are said to you.

ip	**iss**	**ix**
a. _____	a. _____	a. _____
b. _____	b. _____	b. _____
c. _____		
d. _____		
e. _____		

E. Remember the sound ă makes. Read the following sentences.

1. Nan had a nap.
2. Jack played with Jan.
3. Pam packed.
4. And Hal had some jam.

NUMBER 3: Choose the words from each list in Section D.

F. Circle the sentence that describes the picture.

1.
   a. Jill hits Tim.
   b. Jill kisses Tim.
   c. Jill kicks Tim.

2.
   a. You can see a rib.
   b. You can see a lip.
   c. You can see a hip.

3.
   a. The bag is ripped.
   b. The tip is $1.
   c. Tim fixes the house.

G. Write the word that goes with each picture.

1. _____

2. _____ **6**

3. _____

4. _____

H. How are you doing?

In this section you answered 61 questions. Count the number of questions you got wrong and look at the chart to see how you did.

NUMBER WRONG	
0—5	Excellent
6—10	Great
11—15	Very Good
16—21	Good
22—27	OK

DIRECTIONS: When the student is comfortable with this format, similar exercises in later lessons can be assigned for independent work. The answer key is on page 80.

ADDITIONAL REINFORCEMENT: The Advanced Phonics Exercises on pages 75 and 76 can be used with those students who completed Sounding It Out without difficulty.

★ What Is Reading? ★

We asked 6 people to talk about what reading is.

Reading is important. Adults have to know how to read.

Reading is OK. I did not like to read when I was a kid. I like it more as I get older.

Reading is not for me. I like to *do* things. I do not like to read.

Reading is a good way to learn things. When you can read, you do not have to have a teacher.

Reading is knowing what something says, and then thinking about it.

Reading is something that the schools say is important. I do not think it is that important. It gives teachers something to teach.

DIRECTIONS: This section provides reinforcement of the vocabulary and skills presented in this lesson. When the student is comfortable with the format of this section, these exercises can be assigned for independent work.

(67)

1. Read the sentences. Then reread the words in bold print. Find the words in bold print in the box of letters. Words go from left to right and top to bottom.

j	p	q	u	f	v
a	f	r	a	i	d
s	g	e	t	r	x
k	b	c	d	s	y
f	e	l	t	z	
m	o	t	h	e	r
z	w	o	m	a	n

a. I know that **woman**.
b. She is a good **mother**.
c. **First** we have to go.
d. How do you **feel**?
e. Did you **get** it?
f. I will **ask** her.
g. Rick is **afraid** to go.

2. Unscramble the following sentences.

   Example:

   pigs afraid of Kim is.   Kim <u>is afraid of pigs</u>.

   a. mother My book a reads.   My _____

   b. Jill good feels.   Jill _____

   c. The wig a woman has.   The _____

   d. was She girlfriend my first.   She _____

   e. play my pals with I.   I _____

3. Write your own tongue twister. Use the following words and any others you need.

   friend   for   fight   family   fun   fat   free
   fill   from   feel   fib   fit   fin   fig   first   fix

   Example: <u>My friend's family is free from fat and feels fit—no fibbing</u>.

   _____

   _____

DIRECTIONS: After explaining these exercises to the student, assign them as independent work. The answer key is on page 80.

1. Decide which word should go in the _____. Then write it.

   a. **Baby** is to **bib**

      as

      woman is to _____ .

      say pin

   b. **House** is to **live**

      as

      money is to _____ .

      spend fix

2. What do you think? Spend some time thinking about your answer before you circle it.

   a. It is OK to be fat.   Yes   No   Maybe

   b. It is OK to get high.   Yes   No   Maybe

   c. It is OK to be afraid.   Yes   No   Maybe

3. Put an X on the word that does not belong in the column.

a.	read	c.	How?	e.	asked	g.	hip
	write		Why?		played		rib
	hip		What?		wanted		lip
			place		world		work

b.	yell	d.	mitt	f.	more	h.	jam
	talk		bat		most		ham
	to		you		many		get
	gab				tan		

4. Who do you think wrote these sentences? Read the first sentence. Then guess who wrote it. Circle your answer. Spend some time thinking about why you circled one and not another. Do the other sentences in the same way.

   a. I think school is a waste.   a little boy   a woman   cannot tell

   b. I wrote a book on how to fix things.   a man   a woman   cannot tell

   c. I want to get married.   a man   a woman   cannot tell

DIRECTIONS: Read the directions for each section. Exercise 1 covers analogies, item sets that are similar in some way. Exercise 3 concerns classification; the student should establish a relationship between the items, then eliminate the unrelated item. In exercises 2 and 4 the student makes inferences about his or her reading. Examples for each of these exercises might be helpful to the student. As the student becomes comfortable with these exercises, they can be assigned as independent work. The answer key for exercises 1 and 3 is on page 80.

ON YOUR OWN

★ The Best Brother ★

When I was little I did not like my brother, Pat. I was jealous of him. Dad used to tell him that he was his "best boy."

Dad used to spend all his time with his "best boy." He had no time to spend with me. I wanted Dad to do things with me, but he was always teaching "best boy" to talk and do other things. "Best boy" was slow at learning.

When I was 7 and Pat was 8, Dad used to make me play with "best boy." He wanted me to work on teaching him to talk. I did not want to teach "best boy" anything. Sometimes when Dad was not looking, I hit my brother.

"Best boy" did not have any friends at all. At 10, he did not talk. He was slow at thinking. He did not go to school.

At 37, Pat does not talk and he is slow at most things. He cannot do the things that you and I do. He cannot go to work. His world is the house.

I have worked at teaching Pat to talk. He cannot learn, but I have learned the most important thing from him. I have learned to love. Dad's best boy has become my best brother.

★ Love and Other Things ★

Your kisses give me a kick.

I love you as a brother;
I love you as a mother;
I love you as a friend;
I love you as a lover;
I love you as I have not loved before.

I loved you when we were kids.
I loved you when we married.
I loved you when we had kids.
I love you more and more all the time.

Some people play with love
like children play tag.

At 11, a boy likes having a girlfriend like he likes housework.
At 21, a boy likes having a girlfriend and a house that he likes.

Love comes quietly
and plays on my mind,
making you into something
I have to have.

I have all that I want,
I have you.

I look at you
and want to tell you
of my love,
but my bossy mind
tells me
to be quiet.

 TWO READING EXERCISES: These exercises provide reinforcement and can be assigned as independent work.

MORE READING

★ The Rappills ★

SID

I am a boss at the mill. I like most things about being a boss. The money is good. I like telling people what to do. But sometimes I have to sack people. Then I feel bad.

I am married to Pat. I was 20 when we married. Pat was 18.

When I was 20, most of my friends were getting married. I wanted to get married, too. Pat said that she loved me. But she did not want to get married. She wanted to go to school. She was good in school.

I used to sit and think about getting married. Then I talked to Pat's dad. He liked me. I talked to Pat's mother. She liked me, too. They talked to Pat. She said OK.

When we married, things were not too good. I worked at the mill. But I did not make good money. Pat had a baby. We had to live with Pat's mother and dad.

But then the boss asked me to fix things in the lab. The money was good. Pat went back to school. She had another child. And things are good. We have a house. We have some money. We have 2 lovely girls.

I like having girls. But sometimes I want to have a boy. Maybe we will have another child.

MORE READING: This story provides reinforcement and can be assigned as independent work after Lesson 5 is finished.

PAT

I am a teacher and a mother. I married Sid when I was 18. At first I did not want to get married. I wanted to see places and do things. I wanted to see the world. I wanted to become the first woman president.

But then my mother and dad talked to me. They did not want me to go to school. They said they had no money for my schooling. Not many girls went past high school then.

Mother and Dad wanted me to get married. They said that Sid was a good man.

I said OK to Sid. I got a job at the mill. But I had Jane when I was 19. I did not work then. We lived with my mother and dad. That was bad for me. My mother was always telling me what to do. I love her but sometimes she is a nag.

When Jane was 3, I went back to work. Sid worked from 7 a.m. to 7 p.m. in the lab. We had money. We picked out a big house. Then I went back to school. We had another little girl, too.

I liked school and I did OK. I am a teacher. I make good money, and I like what I do.

I like having 2 girls. I like being married. But I will not make my kids get married.

Jane is 13. She loves school. She loves to read. I want her to get all the schooling she can. Then maybe she will get to see the world. Or maybe she will become the first woman president.

JANE

I am 13. I love my family. My dad is my best friend. He is like a big kid. Sometimes we play tag. All my girlfriends say he is good looking. My mother is OK, too. She loves to read. Sometimes she reads the books I read. Then we talk about them. She likes me to get A's. She is a teacher. She thinks school is important. I do too.

I do not have a boyfriend. Sometimes I think I want one. But it is OK not having one. I have many girlfriends.

★ The Bookmans ★

ANN

I am married to Will and we have one child. Dan, my boy, is 14. Will works at the high school. He fixes things. He likes his work. Sometimes I work.

We wanted to have more children. I wanted to have a little girl. But I was older when we married.

I did not work before I married. I lived with my mother. She was sickly. I did things for her. I read to her. I made her jam. I wrote to people for her. I did all the housework.

When I was little, my mother was good to me. She was a good woman in other ways, too. I loved her and liked her. She did not get to see Dan. I feel bad about that. She passed away before I married Will.

Dan is a good boy. Like his Dad, he is quiet. He likes to fix things. But he is like me in some ways, too. People say he looks like me. I love music and he loves music. He is learning how to play the sax.

WILL

I work in the high school. It is a good place to work. I like the kids and the teachers. The other six workers are good people, too.

I do not have money. But I have the important things. I have good friends. I have work that I like. I am married, and I have a child.

I married 2 times. The first woman I married was a nag. All she wanted was money. But she did not work. She wanted me to give her things.

She was jealous, too. She did not want me to see my family. We had no friends. We had many fights. It was like World War III all the time.

It was a good thing that she did not want kids. She ran away with Bill Pags. I did not feel bad. Not at all!

Ann's family and my family were friends. I always liked Ann. But we were not good friends. Her mother was sickly. She lived with her mother.

When her mother passed away, I asked Ann out. I knew she was a good woman. I asked her to get married.

We have a boy. Dan is 14. He looks like his mother. But in other ways he is like me. He likes to fix things. Sometimes he goes to the high school with me. We have a good time.

DAN

I am getting older. I do not like to play with little kids—or do little kid things. I like to do things with my dad. Sometimes I work with him. He is teaching me how to fix things.

I do OK in school. I do not love it. But I do OK.

My mother thinks school is important. My mother is OK for a mother. She is teaching me how to read music. I am learning how to play the sax. Maybe that is what I will do someday—play the sax for money.

Advanced Phonics Exercises

Lesson 3

A. Read each of the following words. The words that are marked by an asterisk are nonsense words.

pit	hit	bit	lid	did		pick	sick
wit	fit	kit	hid	kid		kick	tick
sit	lit	* dit	bid	rid		Rick	lick
it	* rit		Sid	* id		* ick	Nick

B. Review the ă word families.

cab	gab		bat	fat	mat	cap
jab	tab		rat	cat	pat	lap
lab	* zab		sat	hat	* zat	rap
nab			at	* wat		

C. Apply what you know about word families to longer words.

vis it	Will you **visit** me?
rap id	He ran **rapidly**.
pic nic	Do you want to go on a **picnic**?
rab bit	The child has a **rabbit**.
tim id	She is **timid**.
at tic	What is in the **attic**?

Lesson 4

A. Read each of the following words. The words that are marked by an asterisk are nonsense words.

pin	* zin	him	dim	pill	fill	ill	rid
win	in	rim	* bim	will	kill	Jill	Sid
tin	kin	Tim		bill	hill	mill	* id
fin		* lim		* nill	* zill	* rill	

PURPOSE: The Advanced Phonics Exercises are for students who completed Sounding It Out without difficulty. They show the student how to decode words that are phonically regular. The Advanced Phonics Exercises are correlated to Lessons 3, 4, and 5.
DIRECTIONS: Explain the purpose of this exercise and inform the student that nonsense words will be used to see how well he or she has learned the word families in the previous lessons. The nonsense words have asterisks next to them.

B. Review the **ă** word families.

lap	cap	bad	pad	ran	Hal	cab
nap	gap	dad	ad	ban	Val	jab
rap	* wap	had	* gad	tan	pal	* hab
				* san	* tal	

C. Apply what you know about word families to longer words.

nap kin   Give me a **napkin**.
hab it   I have a bad **habit**.
val id   It is **valid**.
lim it   Do you know the **limit**?
ad dict   He is an **addict**.
ban dit   The **bandit** wanted my money.

Lesson 5

A. Read each of the following words. The words that are marked by an asterisk are nonsense words.

bib	big	mix	miss	rip
rib	wig	six	kiss	hip
* ib	rig	fix	* iss	lip
	* ig	* ix		* kip

B. Review the **ă** word families.

pan	sax	Sam	Pam	back	lack
van	wax	ham	ram	Jack	rack
can	tax	am	* gam	sack	tack
* lan	* fax	* bam		* ack	* kack

C. Apply what you know about word families to longer words.

pan ic   Do not **panic**.
fan a tic   He is a **fanatic**.
tit-for-tat   He believes in **tit-for-tat**.
At lan tic   Did you see the **Atlantic**?

Answer Key

Lesson 1

Quiz
—page 3

B. 1. no
   2. no
   3. no
   4. yes

Skill Building
—pages 4-5

A. read
   to
B. 1. (boy)(friend)
   2. (be)(come)
C. fort
   form
D. of who or
E. 1. more
   2. good
   3. way
   4. come
   5. Of
   6. who
   7. or
F. 1. fight
   2. fighter

   3. teacher
   4. teach
G. them then
H. 1. come
   2. way

Sounding It Out
—pages 8-10

B. 1. rib
   2. kiss
   3. lips
D. 1. his
   2. in
   3. if
E. will is children
F. 2. a. hid
      b. will
      c. kid
      d. Sid
      e. did
      f. bill
      g. Jill
G. 1. c
   2. b
   3. a
H. 1. hill
   2. pill
   3. lid

Playing with Words
—page 12

1.
```
x  g (w  a  y) y
(c  o  m  e) b
j (o  r) z  i
k (d  w  h  o)
(m  o  r  e) f
```

2. a. He is a bad boy.
   b. Pam is a teacher.
   c. Sal is not a child.
   d. My cat likes to play.
   e. Is she going?

Thinking with Words
—page 13

1. a. men
   b. go
3. a. mill
   b. then
   c. you
   d. good

Lesson 2

Quiz
—page 18

B. 1. no
   2. no
   3. yes
   4. no
E. a. 2
   b. 1
   c. 3

Skill Building
—pages 19-20

A. learn
   can
B. 1. (out)(come)
   2. (mad)(man)
   3. (mad)(house)
C. call
   fall
D. from was
E. 1. made
   2. was
   3. president
   4. went
   5. from
   6. world
   7. war
F. 1. older
   2. teach
   3. littler
   4. quiet
G. mind yelling do

Sounding It Out
—pages 23-25

B. 1. pill
   2. hip
   3. dig
D. 1. sick
   2. it
E. with little give
F. 2. a. bib
      b. him
      c. Tim Kim
      d. fib
G. 1. b
   2. b
   3. b
H. 1. rib
   2. bib

Playing with Words
—page 27

1.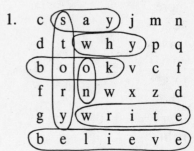

2. a. Tim loves Pam.
   b. They learn in the lab.
   c. Kim is my best friend.
   d. Married people need more money.
   e. Sam will read to them.

Thinking with Words
—page 28

1. a. girl
   b. man
3. a. use
   b. when
   c. more
   d. housework

Lesson 3

Quiz
—page 32

B. 1. yes
   2. no
   3. no

Skill Building
—pages 33-34

A. people
   Some
B. 1. (kid)(nap)
   2. (back)(pack)
   3. (cat)(nap)
C. hall   call
   mall   tall
D. write   why
E. 1. say
   2. write
   3. book
   4. Why
   5. believe
   6. on
   7. story
F. 1. writer
   2. teacher
   3. sad
   4. higher
G. little   baby

Sounding It Out
—pages 37-39

B. 1. pig
   2. mitt
   3. bib
D. 1. kiss
   2. tip
E. with   will   important
F. 2. a. pick
      b. sick
      c. hit
      d. bit
      e. Rick
      f. sit
H. 1. b
   2. a
   3. b
I. 1. kick
   2. pit
   3. hit

Playing with Words
—page 41

1.
```
c (s  a  y) j  m  n
d  t (w  h  y) p  q
(b  o  o  k) v  c  f
f  r (n) w  x  z  d
g (y (w  r  i  t  e)
(b  e  l  i  e  v  e)
```

2. a. Dan and Nick talk about school.
   b. Jill looks at her map.
   c. Pam wants to be president.
   d. I want to play music.
   e. The school is on a hill.

Thinking with Words
—page 42

1. a. book
   b. your
3. a. friend
   b. pan
   c. learn
   d. hat
   e. think
   f. them

Lesson 4

Quiz
—page 46

B. 1. yes
   2. no
   3. yes
   4. no
E. 3
   2
   1

Skill Building
—pages 47-48

A. are
   good
   at
   people
B. 1. anything
   2. anyway
   3. anyhow
C. warm
   warp
D. that one
E. 1. place
   2. slow
   3. live
   4. that
   5. adult

6. one
7. any
F. 1. friendly
   2. bad
   3. reader
   4. works
   5. writing
   6. quiet
G. money house
H. place

Sounding It Out
—pages 51-53

B. 1. hill
   2. wig
   3. sip
D. 1. miss
   2. win
E. 1. Bill Sid lip
   2. fan hat pack
F. 2. a. win
      b. tin
      c. big
      d. sin
      e. pins OR pigs
H. 1. c
   2. b
   3. b
I. 1. dig
   2. pig
   3. wig

Playing with Words
—page 55

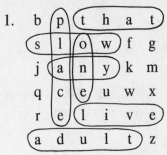

2. a. I like slow music.
   b. Nan made that mat.
   c. Pam likes a quiet place.
   d. Anyone can be president.
   e. Sid wants to work.

Thinking with Words
—page 56

1. a. little
   b. out
3. a. children
   b. van
   c. feel
   d. wig
   e. say
   f. mat

Lesson 5

Skill Building
—pages 60-61

A. like
   read
B. 1. anyone
   2. catnip
   3. into

C. warn
   wart
D. feel get
E. 1. woman
   2. mother
   3. First
   4. feel
   5. get
   6. ask
   7. afraid

F. 1. slow
   2. bigger
   3. friendly
   4. getting
   5. winner
G. best brother
H. mother

Sounding It Out
   —pages 64-66

B. 1. cat
   2. pig
   3. lips
   4. pan
C. 1. family   hand   ask   happen
   2. fill   miss   pick   pit
D. 2. a. kiss
   b. fix
   c. tip
   d. rip
   e. miss
F. 1. b
   2. c
   3. b
G. 1. kiss
   2. six
   3. lips
   4. hip

Playing with Words
   —page 68

1.

2. a. My mother reads a book.
   b. Jill feels good.
   c. The woman has a wig
   d. She was my first girlfriend.
   e. I play with my pals.

Thinking with Words
   —page 69

1. a. pin
   b. spend
3. a. hip
   b. to
   c. place
   d. you
   e. world
   f. tan
   g. work
   h. get

Word List

Uses of Word List: The Word List has three basic uses. 1) For students who resist testing, the Word List can be used to determine whether or not Book 2 is appropriate for the student. 2) Prior to assigning independent work in Book 2, the instructor can examine the Word List to ensure that the student knows a high percentage of the words. 3) The instructor can use the Word List as a resource for creating additional reinforcement activities.

Groundbreaker Exercises

Lesson 1	Lesson 2	Lesson 3	Lesson 4	Lesson 5	Lesson 6	Lesson 7
love	house	play	boy	talk	they	quiet
work	school	music	girl	fight	are	people
like	time	friend	child	old	money	jealous
do	think	for	children	me	yell	most
does	read	thing	the	her	married	may
not	go	have	is	will	about	look
he	to	see	can	she	with	make
you	too		want			

Book 1

Lesson 1

and	bat	ban
family	cat	can
some	fat	Dan
all	hat	fan
little	mat	Jan
we	pat	man
tell	rat	Nan
	sat	pan
	that	ran
		tan

Lesson 2

how	gal	bag
mind	Hal	gag
be	pal	hag
know	Sal	lag
then		nag
waste		rag
high		tag
		wag

Lesson 3

boss	bad	Max
bossy	dad	tax
important	had	wax
men	lad	
teach	mad	
teacher	pad	
my	sad	
best		
use		

Lesson 4

spend	back	cap
brother	Jack	gap
give	lack	lap
then	pack	map
many	rack	nap
but	sack	rap
other	tack	sap
		tap

Lesson 5

free	cab	cam	bass
baby	dab	dam	lass
out	gab	ham	mass
your	jab	jam	pass
learn	lab	Pam	
what	nab	ram	
when	tab	Sam	

Book 2

Lesson 1

come	bid	bill
way	did	fill
or	hid	hill
good	kid	Jill
who	lid	kill
of	rid	mill
more	Sid	pill
		till
		will

Lesson 2

president	bib	dim
was	fib	him
were	jib	Jim
world	rib	rim
made		Tim
war		vim
went		Kim
from		

Lesson 3

book	Dick	bit
on	kick	fit
write	lick	hit
say	Mick	kit
story	Nick	lit
stories	pick	pit
believe	quick	quit
why	Rick	sit
	sick	wit

Lesson 4

one	bin	big
that	fin	dig
live	pin	fig
slow	sin	pig
adult	tin	rig
place	win	wig
any		

Lesson 5

woman	dip	kiss	fix
women	hip	miss	mix
feel	lip		
mother	rip		
get	ship		
ask	sip		
afraid	tip		
first			

NOTE: The words in boxes are the new words presented in each lesson. The other words are based on the word families in Sounding It Out.

Getting Ready

You can use the words and word finds below to prepare for the posttest. You can do this by reading the words before you find them. If you cannot read a word, go to the lesson where it is introduced or ask your instructor to help you. Remember that the words in the word find go from left to right and from top to bottom.

Lesson 1

w	h	o	m	x	c
a	g	o	o	d	o
y	z	f	r	o	m
x	o	r	e	r	e

come   who

way   of

or   more

good

Lesson 2

z	q	x	w	e	n	t	z	g
b	u	f	w	e	r	e	b	h
c	v	r	a	w	a	r	c	j
g	x	o	s	m	a	d	e	k
h	y	m	w	o	r	l	d	q
p	r	e	s	i	d	e	n	t

president   was

were   went

world   from

made   war

Lesson 3

b	w	h	y	w	f	j
o	s	t	o	r	y	k
o	a	x	n	i	g	m
k	y	z	c	t	h	q
b	e	l	i	e	v	e

book   story

on   believe

write   why

say

Lesson 4

a	d	u	l	t
s	l	o	w	h
x	i	n	a	a
z	v	e	n	t
g	e	f	y	r
p	l	a	c	e

one   adult

that   place

live   any

slow

Lesson 5

b	x	f	e	e	l
c	z	i	g	e	t
a	f	r	a	i	d
j	a	s	k	x	y
m	o	t	h	e	r
p	w	o	m	a	n

woman   ask

feel   afraid

mother   first

get

Book 2 Posttest

1. Read these sentences.

   a. Jill bit the pit.
   b. Dick kicked him.
   c. Did Kim miss Nick?
   d. Kim hid it on the hill.

   e. Will you fix the lid?
   f. The pig made me sick.
   g. Tim digs with a pick.

2. Read this story.

   Jim,

   I feel like I know you. I read your first book on presidents of the U.S.A. Then I read your story on World War II.

   You know what you are talking about. All thinking adults are afraid of another war.

   I have to ask you one thing. Will you be writing another book? When? And on what?

   If you have time, you can write me at:
   >   23 Good Way
   >   Motherly, New Jersey   099550

   >   Rick Faks

3. Say these words.

   a. come
   b. woman
   c. get

   d. or
   e. from

4. What sound does **short i** make? What word helps you remember this sound?

5. Say these words.

   a. slower
   b. player

   c. fatter
   d. worker

   e. higher
   f. fighter

   g. older

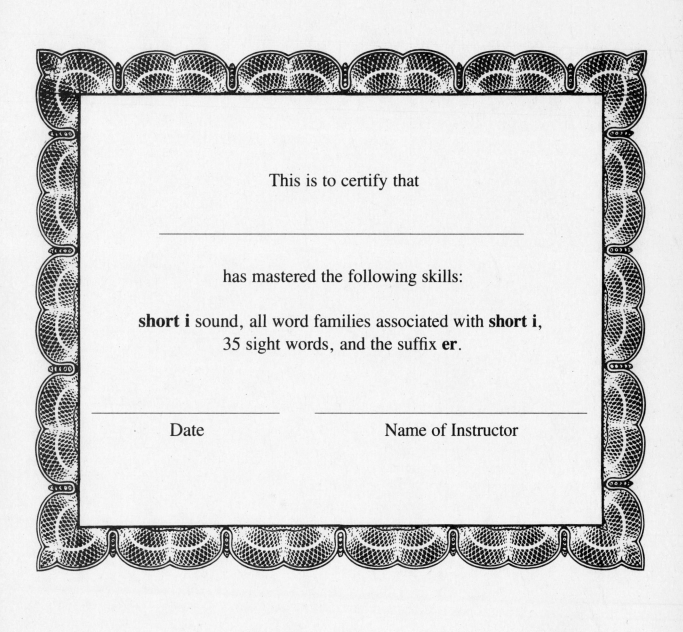

This is to certify that

_____

has mastered the following skills:

short i sound, all word families associated with **short i**,
35 sight words, and the suffix **er**.

_____   _____
Date   Name of Instructor

book	war	went	was	who	way
write	world	president	made	of	good
say	from	were	or	come	more

INSTRUCTIONS FOR USE OF FLASH CARDS: After the student has completed a lesson, cut out the flash cards for that lesson. Show the student the side of the card that has only the word. Separate those words he or she misreads from those words that he or she reads correctly. The student should be instructed to use the picture and sentence on the back of the card as a memory aid for the word.

Are you going my **way**?

Matt is a **good** man.

I want **more** money.

Who is she?

They are 4 **of** my friends.

I want you to **come** with me.

He **was** my friend.

I **made** him go.

Are the boys **or** girls going?

The girl **went** to work.

She is **president**.

They **were** going to school.

Do you want to go to **war**?

The **world** is big.

We will go **from** her house.

I want to read the **book**.

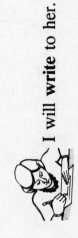

I will **write** to her.

He likes to **say** that he is important.

afraid	ask	get
feel	first	mother
woman	any	one
adult	that	live
slow	place	story
on	believe	why

INSTRUCTIONS FOR USE OF FLASH CARDS: After the student has completed a lesson, cut out the flash cards for that lesson. Show the student the side of the card that has only the word. Separate those words he or she misreads from those words that he or she reads correctly. The student should be instructed to use the picture and sentence on the back of the card as a memory aid for the word.

The boy is **on** the hill.

Many people **believe** in him.

Why is he going?

Most people are **slow** at learning something.

SLOW

Do you have a **place** to go?

I will tell you a **story**.

He is an **adult**.

I will see **that** she goes to school.

I **live** in a big house.

I know that **woman**.

Will you see **any** friends?

#1 She has **one** baby.

How do you feel?

First we have to go.

She is a good **mother**.

Rick is **afraid** to go.

I will **ask** her.

Did you **get** it?